Untucked

REFLECTIONS FOR
THE SOUL'S
UNFOLDING

Jeannine Lindstrom

Published by Tuck the Fringe, LLC, Kansas City, MO

Book Cover by David Provolo
Photo by Saige Gilmore

ISBN (paperback) 979-8-9942235-0-5
ISBN (ebook) 979-8-9942235-1-2

First edition 2026

Published in the United States of America

Inquires: hello@tuckthefringe.com

The reflections, stories, and insights shared in this book are offered from the author's personal experience and perspective. While care has been taken to ensure the accuracy of information presented, the author makes no guarantees regarding completeness or applicability to individual circumstances. This book is not intended as medical, psychological, legal, or professional advice.

Quotations from other authors and sources are included for educational and inspirational purposes. Every effort has been made to attribute quotations accurately. These quotations are believed to fall under fair use. Some quotations were obtained through publicly available internet sources, and no indication was found that permission was required at the time of use. Any errors or omissions are unintentional.

For my grandson, Lawler.
May you always know the true nature
of your own spirit.

Table of Contents

Prologue

Intermission

The stage lights dim. The curtain falls. Applause erupts like a wave.

But I don't move.

I can't.

"What just happened?"

I said it out loud, but it was just a whisper. My mind races, but the words won't come. My pulse is still pounding from the last scene, yet everyone around me is already standing, stretching, chatting as if nothing happened. Like they weren't just swept up in a whirlwind of emotion. Am I the only one still reeling?

Those first two acts had me on the edge of my seat, holding my breath and feeling emotions I didn't even realize I had.

Now what? Am I supposed to just... pause? Shake it off like the others, grab a drink, stretch my legs? Or do I sit here, heart pounding, replaying every scene, letting it all sink in?

The actors didn't just perform, they truly lived every moment. Every breath, pause, and crack in their voices felt authentic, as if I weren't just watching but experiencing it myself. The tension, heartbreak, and unexpected betrayals, I felt them all, deep in my chest. I was there, inside the story, lost in the chaos. Then… intermission. Just as I was clutching the edge of my seat, the momentum was suddenly taken away. Now what?

A forced pause. A break I didn't ask for. A moment of nothing in the middle of everything.

How long does this last? Fifteen minutes? Thirty?

And more importantly… what comes next?

I glance down at the playbill rolled up in my hands. I flip it open, and suddenly I'm not reading a synopsis. I'm reading my life.

Jeannine lived an 'acceptable' life.

Acceptable. The word sits heavy in my heart.

If acceptance is earned through people-pleasing, codependency, hypervigilance, and overachieving. If being 'acceptable' means walking on eggshells, molding yourself to fit spaces never meant for you. A round peg in a square hole, trying so hard to belong, never stopping to ask, *Do I even want to?*

Acceptable? At what cost?

Intermission…

The place between who I was and who I'm becoming…

Introduction

"The privilege of a lifetime is to become
who you truly are." —Carl Jung

There is a moment right after the curtain falls, right before the lights come back on, when something in you refuses to return to who you were before.

That's where this book begins.

In the pause.

In the awakening.

In the quiet space between the life you lived and the life you're finally ready to claim.

At first, this shift feels like a whisper, a restlessness you can't quite name. The sense that the armor you've worn for years, maybe decades, has become too heavy. You're tired of playing roles that were never truly yours—tired of shrinking, apologizing, and softening your voice just to fit in. Deep down, you know you can't keep living a half-lived life. The cost of that is far too high.

You start to sense the burden of the *shoulds* and the pull of something deeper.

That's the beginning of Untucking.

This book reflects my own journey into that place. *Untucked.* It feels like a lifetime in the making. What I share here comes from decades of journaling my thoughts, prayers, meditations, and conversations with God.

The title *Untucked* naturally evolved from the phrase *Tuck the Fringe.* That phrase was born in my yoga class in 2013 when I asked my students to fold their blankets neatly for a restorative posture and to "tuck the fringe." It caught on. Soon I was saying it often, and when I didn't, my students said it for me. Then one day, as I gave the instruction, I realized I had been metaphorically "tucking the fringe" my whole life: conforming, pleasing, fitting myself into a neat little package. A realization that was so profound that it started shaping not only my writing but also my healing.

I started writing this book as I came out of what I affectionately call my Intermission. An unexpected six-year pause that started when I was 49. Unexpected, but completely necessary to heal from a lifetime of hiding to meet expectations that never truly belonged to me. Intermission wasn't glamorous. It was quiet, often lonely, and deeply sacred. I was grieving who I thought I was. I was learning to listen to the voice beneath the noise, the one that had been mine all along.

I call it **SELF-uncovery**: a return to what you once knew before shame rewrote your worth, before performance shaped your identity, before you tucked your SELF away.

Maybe you're here because something inside you is awakening.

Maybe life broke you open, and now you're looking for what is real.

You don't have to believe as I do. You don't need to name God as I do. You only need a willingness to meet what is true for you. Bring your faith, your doubt, your joy, your grief. There is room for all of it here.

These reflections are threads in my own tapestry, woven with questions, wonderings, moments of ache, and moments of awe. Rooted in faith and drawn from experience, they come in the form of meditations, journal entries, prayers, and poems that emerged as I learned to Untuck. They flow directly from my journal pages and read as such, sometimes full of depth and sometimes choppy and direct.

There are four sections: **Stillness Speaks, The Courage to Rise, Sacred Belonging, and Nature Heals.** Each represents a season of my soul.

These words are meant to meet you softly where you are and remind you that you're not alone as you untuck and return to your truest SELF.

Every reflection includes a **Whisper**, a kind of mantra, followed by a **Prompt** to help you connect with your own experience. The prompts may invite you to journal, pause, or simply notice what emerges within you.

I wrote this book to be read in any order you choose.

Open it wherever you feel led. Let your heart be your guide. No matter how you move through it, remember this: these words no longer belong to me. They are now yours.

Let this be a devotional for your soul's unfolding.

Take what you need. Return whenever your heart calls you back.

You are not alone here, and you were never meant to stay tucked.

J~

Section I

Stillness Speaks

Stillness Speaks is a refuge for silence, soul pauses, and re-orientation.

In a world that moves quickly and demands much of our attention, stillness can feel like a rare and treasured gift. It is within stillness that we find the space to breathe deeply, listen inward, and reconnect with the parts of ourselves often hidden beneath noise, distraction, and expectation.

What if stillness is not emptiness but the memory of where we began?

What if presence is how the soul remembers where it belongs?

This section invites you to step away from busyness, rest and return to the quiet center where your soul can settle and your heart can open. Through gentle reflections, you'll be guided to cultivate presence, peace, and compassion for yourself as you begin to untuck the layers that have kept you from fully living your truth.

This is where healing begins and the Divine whispers. I invite you to slow down, soften, and remember that you are enough just as you are in each moment.

The Gift of Rest

Reflection:

It used to take sickness to throw me into rest because I would never choose it on my own. Whenever my ego ignored the signs to stop pushing play, God lovingly pressed pause. What initially felt like collapse or failure was really divine rest hidden under a forced stop.

When my body and spirit had nothing left to give, I was forced to lay down the hustle. Rest was no longer just something I squeezed in after work; it became the work itself. Time carved out without demands or expectations.

At first, it felt like weakness, even failure. But gradually I started to see what God was doing: removing false identities, loosening my attachment to busyness, and stripping away the armor I had mistaken for strength.

Rest is often the first thread we loosen when we begin to untuck ourselves, revealing the truth that thick skin is not a badge of honor. Healing doesn't come from pushing harder but from surrendering. And surrender begins with rest.

Even now, I sometimes want to retreat into that neat

little package, to tuck myself away again. That's when the message gets louder: stop hustling, stop fixing, stop trying to prove myself. Just rest.

So I'm learning to see rest as a sacred return, where God does His deepest work.

Whisper

"My soul finds rest in God alone; my salvation comes from him. He alone is my rock and my salvation; he is my fortress, I will never be shaken." — Psalm 62:1–2

Journal Prompt

Where in your life are you confusing hustle with strength? What might God be asking you to let go of so you can finally find true rest?

Come to Me ~ A Meditation

"Come to me, all you who are weary and burdened,
and I will give you rest.
Take my yoke upon you and learn from me,
for I am gentle and humble in heart,
and you will find rest for your souls."
— Matthew 11:28–29

Reflection:
When your energy wanes, rest in the everlasting arms of the Holy Spirit.
Be gentle with yourself.
Trust in your unbreakable connection to God.

Take my yoke upon you...
Allow yourself to become still.
Bring awareness to your breath.
Invite stillness into your body.
Become the observer of your thoughts,
letting them rise and fall
like waves with each breath.

Come to me, all who are weary and burdened.
Begin to let go of distractions.
Lay down judgment.
Give yourself permission
to be fully present with God in this moment.
You don't need words
the words have already been spoken.
The sacred is within you,
as you gently drop into your heart.
Allow joy to enter.
Let grace rise.

Humble in heart
Find the quietness in this sacred space.
Let go of what you carry.
Surrender to the peace already within you.
Embrace the gentle guidance
drawing you inward,
where the Holy Spirit's embrace holds you tenderly.
In this moment,
allow yourself to simply *be*
attuned to the sacredness within.

Breathe here awhile.
You are home.

Whisper:
*You don't need to earn rest. You are deserving of peace
exactly as you are.*

Prompt:

What does it mean for you to "come home" to yourself?

20

Return to Solitude

Reflection:

"Be still, and know that I am God." – Psalm 46:10

Looking back at my timeline, I realize there was never a time when I truly lived alone until I was 49 and recently divorced. It was the first time the house felt quiet. In an unfamiliar way. It wasn't just the absence of others; it was the sudden presence of myself.

At first, the silence was deafening. There were no voices calling my name, no footsteps down the hall, and no background noise from daily life. It was just me. The walls felt like they were listening.

And in that stillness, I started to hear what I hadn't allowed myself to feel in years. My longings and doubts. My dreams and grief.

That season of solitude became a turning point, and I chose to meet myself there. What I feared as emptiness transformed into sacred ground.

What if, instead of avoiding solitude, I embraced trusting that on the other side I would emerge wiser, clearer, and more whole?

Whisper:

God, help me not to fear the silence, but to meet You in it.

Thank You for the courage to be truly present with myself and for reminding me that in solitude, I return to my most natural self, the one You created with care and purpose.

When the silence feels overwhelming, remind me that I am never alone.

When I long for noise to distract me, help me stay present long enough to hear Your whisper.

Let this stillness be more than just absence. Let it become communion.

Teach me to trust the unfolding, to embrace the sacred in the pause, and to recognize that even in stillness, You are working within me.

Prompt:

What parts of yourself have you rediscovered in quiet moments?

What could still be waiting to be heard?

Wise Use of Time

Reflection:

"The medicine for hurry is presence. The cure for scarcity is awareness."—Jacob Nordby *The Creative Cure*

What is time, really, other than another way to measure? So often, we hear people say, *"I don't have enough time."* But is that true? Maybe we don't use it wisely.

I don't believe that using our time wisely involves squeezing productivity out of every minute or becoming strict with schedules. It means becoming aware and shifting our beliefs about time by being mindful in the moment.

Every moment questions: How will I use my time? How will I show up?

Slowing down is always a conscious choice. Just one awakened moment is enough to transform the quality of time.

Sometimes it means taking a deep breath instead of reacting in a challenging situation. Other times, it involves stepping away from the constant noise of social media to build more meaningful connections. For me, it means starting each day with prayer, reflection, and meditation.

Living consciously isn't always easy. Old habits pull us back into busyness and distraction. But when the world feels chaotic, and all seems lost, we can start again with just a single breath. And then another.

We truly can slow down time if we decide to.

Whisper:

Time is not your enemy. Slow down and let it expand with your awareness.

Prompt:

Think about how you relate to time. Do you often feel rushed or distracted?

What would it look like to slow down time through awareness?

Write about a small daily choice you could make to live more present and connected to your SELF.

On the Edge

Reflection:

Find yourself in the stillness of your breath. Let your awareness gently settle on the edge of your being where your inner world meets the outer world. This is the threshold between self and surroundings, the quiet boundary where you hold both presence and possibility.

As you breathe in, feel the gentle pulse of your Spirit at this edge, vibrant and alive. Throughout life's journey, as the core of your soul becomes stronger, a natural desire arises to release what no longer serves you and return to a place of stillness and quiet grounding.

What once protected you like a suit of armor served its purpose well. It guarded your tender heart from harm and kept you safe through storms. But over time, that protective shell grew thick and heavy, becoming less a shield and more a barrier that stifles growth and dulls sensation.

It takes courage to face what has long been your refuge and vulnerability to step into the unknown. These worn defenses have kept you numb and safe from pain but also from joy, connection, and true aliveness.

In silence and stillness, you begin to sense the subtle stirrings of your heart and the gentle unfolding of your true self again. As you breathe, quietly offer this prayer to your soul.

Whisper:

Help me shed what I no longer need. Help me feel the sacred edge where You and I meet.

Prompt:

What is one piece of "armor" you've outgrown but still find hard to let go of?

How might stillness help you start to release it?

Drifting Away

Reflection:

I don't always notice when I'm drifting. One moment, I feel connected and grounded in trust, and the next, I'm handling everything myself, unaware that I've slipped into autopilot.

It's not intentional. Just as the earth gently turns away from the sun each night, I, too, have unknowingly drifted away from God. Moving through the hours without awareness or purpose. I didn't even realize it until I felt the distance.

Still, I've seen enough of God's grace not to forget for long. His love is woven through my life's story, in quiet rescues, unexpected mercy, and moments of peace that come when I finally surrender.

Yes, I am human. I will drift, but now I try to notice more quickly. I pause. I breathe. I return.

Because I was never supposed to do this alone.

Whisper:

Holy Spirit, forgive me for the times I've moved without you. When I forget your presence, remind me gently. When I stray, bring me home. Help me live awake, trust you, and stay close.

Prompt:

Can you recall a moment when you realized you were spiritually "on autopilot"?

What helped you return to the presence of God?

How might you incorporate small pauses throughout the day to realign?

When the Mask Cracks

Reflection:

"The wound is the place where the Light enters you."—Rumi

There are times when the most honest prayers spill out in unexpected places, like in a parked car, in the quiet of the night, or under the hot spray of a shower. No polished words. Just truth. Ache. A whisper to something greater than yourself.

After carrying grief and holding onto the persona of the capable one, the "go-to" girl, I cracked open. I didn't plan to; it just happened.

I whispered, "God, if you're there, please help me let go of this heaviness."

What was answered back louder than thought was: *You're already letting go...*

It was as if everything fell away. The unspoken sadness and the version of myself I didn't even realize I was hiding from. That simple, honest cry was a prayer to live in a way that would let me be fully seen.

This moment wasn't a breakdown. It was an unveiling. A baptism in truth. Not dramatic or loud, but very clear.

When I finally voiced the pain I'd been carrying, God didn't scold me. He whispered back, *You're already becoming.*

I could feel not only God but also the eyes of those who love me, watching from beyond. They could see past the mask, and that awareness was enough for me to start over.

Whisper:

You don't have to wait for your world to collapse to face a moment of truth. But when it happens, embrace it. Let it mark your new beginning.

Prompt:

If someone you loved could see your life unfiltered, what might they gently encourage you to change?

What Now?

Reflection:

God, please open my eyes to what's next. I am so grateful for the push forward out of a dark season, but now what?

I woke up today, and I didn't even recognize myself. That's scary! How can that be?

There is so much noise around me right now. Well-meaning advice guides me in different directions, and sometimes, if I'm honest, it paralyzes me.

If I am really going to do this, how do I quiet the noise so I can truly find myself?

Deep in my heart, I know it comes from moments of stillness, and I am so grateful for that time each day. Then the world begins to speak!

More than anything, I am excited to untuck this girl. I think she is special! But there are so many questions:

Who am I now if I am not all the roles I've played in the past?

What do I truly value in my life? What brings me joy?

Please, God, guard my heart so I can experience You

and what is truly mine. Waking up from that dark night and feeling this newfound freedom was a frightening journey, but I am here now, and I don't want old patterns to pull me back.

How will I know? What's next? Please show me.

Whisper:

"Be patient toward all that is unsolved in your heart and try to love the questions themselves."—Rainer Maria Rilke

Prompt:

What questions are stirring in your heart right now?
Instead of rushing for answers, write them down as your companions.

Centering Soul

Reflection:

The soul often feels hidden beneath layers of effort. Yet when we create, whether with words, paint, clay, or simply the quiet rhythm of breath, we touch that deep core. Creation isn't about making something perfect. It's about letting what lives inside come to the surface, reminding us that our soul is always there, waiting to be connected with.

Centering Souls - A Poem

You might ask, How do you find the center of the soul?
It's different from asking, "How many licks does it take to reach the Tootsie Roll center of a Tootsie Pop?"
No, it goes much deeper.
Below the mind, beneath the body
Lives the soul.
Yet the body's armor
And the mind's chemical storm
Make the soul seem distant.

How can I dig deep enough to discover the center of my soul?
In the softness of a brushstroke
In the rhythm of music,
In the curve of clay,
In the dance of words,
I meet myself again
Revealing pieces of my soul to the light.
In the stillness of making, my soul awakens
In the courage of creating, my soul starts to rise.
And in this rising, I find my center.
The sweet center of the soul

Whisper:

"Besides being fun, creativity offers a path out of stagnation, unhappiness, self-judgment, and the kind of robotic living that leaves so many of us feeling unfulfilled. Creativity is a forgotten cure."—Jacob Norby *Creative Cure*

Prompt:

Where do you most often feel the "center" of your soul? Choose a simple act of creation today, such as writing, drawing, cooking, singing, or moving your body, and notice what stirs within you.

What awakens in the stillness of creating?

A Silent Drive

Reflection:

Open my eyes, Lord, to the beauty of silence.

I feel You speaking to me as I'm gently nudged to spend my drive in stillness.

No book to listen to.

No music to sing along with.

Just me and You, talking.

You show me the beauty ahead on the windshield's screen.

I ask You questions.

I contemplate Your answers.

I laugh with You.

I cry with You.

Mostly, I feel Your embrace.

Have I ever experienced this kind of silence for six hours?

My heart is open to Your grace and peace.

That day, the road became a sanctuary. There were no external voices, no distractions, just the quiet companionship of God in motion. It reminded me that silence isn't the absence of sound; it's the presence of something deeper.

Sometimes we don't need more information; we need less noise.

Sometimes the clearest conversations with the Divine happen when our mouths and devices are quiet, but our hearts are listening.

Whisper:
Sacred silence is never empty; it is filled with God.

Prompt:
When was the last time you welcomed silence into your day?

Solitude As a Pilgrimage

Reflection:

"The soul always knows what to do to heal itself. The challenge is to silence the mind."—Caroline Myss

Solitude is not exile.

It is an invitation. A sacred inward journey where no map is necessary, only courage.

In the quiet, distractions fade away.

No role to play. No audience to impress. No race to win.

This is where the soul begins to speak.

Like Jesus in the wilderness.

Like Buddha beneath the tree.

The great ones did not withdraw to escape the world, but to remember who they were in it.

You are invited to do the same.

To step off the well-worn path of noise and expectation and return to the inner temple

where the truth is simple,

and your presence is enough.

Let silence do what only silence can.
Not punish but purify.
Not isolate but draw close.

Whisper:

I welcome the stillness not as emptiness but as a sacred return to my soul.

Prompt:

What distractions might you need to let go of to truly connect with yourself?

How could solitude become a sacred threshold instead of something to fear?

When Yesterday Comes Knocking

Reflection:

Good morning, God.

I'm thankful for the peaceful beauty of this day, for the sanctuary I've built, and for the time to be still with You.

And yet… I'm struggling.

Today feels heavy. Despite the layers I've shed, the strength I've claimed, and the healing I've walked through, there are still days like this. Days when the past grips me again. When my thoughts spiral, and I begin to question everything I've already overcome.

I know who I am more than ever before. I trust that there is more life, more light, and more unfolding ahead. But the old voices still whisper sometimes. Those that say I'm not enough and those that pull me into doubt.

And I wonder: How long will it take me to get there? Why after months of gratitude and presence, does that dark undertow still find me?

I don't need all the answers today. I only ask for your grace.

Be in my heart, Holy Spirit. Fill the space where my pain once lived and let peace take root again.

Whisper:

Even now, I am healing. Even here, I am held.
Breathe in: I am held. Breathe out: I am healing.

Prompt:

Have you ever had a day when old wounds whispered louder than your present truth?
It doesn't mean you've gone backward; it means you're still human.
Let this moment be a pause, not a verdict.

My True North

Reflection:

The goal of consciousness isn't perfection; it's presence.

And being present is something I must practice.

Every morning, I wake up not to rush, but to reconnect. Before the noise, before the scrolling, before the world takes a piece of me, I give myself back to God.

My morning ritual is non-negotiable. It's where I reconnect with my center and remember who I am beneath everything I carry.

My practice includes prayer, meditation, devotional reading, journaling and movement. But more than any one component, it is the act of returning to quiet, to stillness, to breath that grounds me.

Consciousness, I've learned, is not a fixed destination. It's daily self-uncovering, a stripping away of the layers I've unconsciously picked up.

Some mornings, I arrive joyfully. Other mornings, I come weary or distracted. But I arrive. And that in itself becomes an act of grace.

Every day, I pray:

I am worthy because You created me.

I live my truth and do not tuck my fringe for anyone.

My thoughts, words, and actions come from gratitude, joy, and peace.

My compass. My due north.

It is where I confess. It is where I remember.

It is where I rise.

Whisper:

Meet me in the morning, God, before I forget who I am. Draw me back to the stillness where my spirit remembers its shape.

Prompt:

What would a soul-centered morning look like for you?

My Daily Prayers

I am worthy because you created me! I live my truth and do not tuck my fringe for anyone. My thoughts, words, and actions come from gratitude, joy, and pace. I live in my authenticity, abundance, and divine expression of who I am made to be. I have the courage and intention to live this every day that you give me!

Forgive me when I fall short, in my thoughts and in my words, in what I have done and what I have failed to do. I ask You for forgiveness and grace so that I can move forward in this day as the divine expression you created me to be.

Metta

May I be filled with loving kindness
May I be safe from inner and outer dangers
May I be well in body and mind
May I be at ease and happy

Jeremiah 29:11

For I know the plans I have for you, declares the Lord. Plans
to prosper you and not to harm you. Plans to give you hope
and a future.
If it is meant for me, it will not pass me by.

The Weight and the Wait

Reflection:

"It is such a struggle—has always been—for each of us to settle deep enough into the wait, into the weight till we discover that there's nowhere to go."—Mark Nepo, *The Book of Awakenings*

Waiting is tough. Let's be honest and acknowledge that. Even the most awakened among us find it difficult.

I admit that I prefer a task to focus on, a tool to learn, a box to check. It is my nature. Yet within that nature comes the deeper question: when is my doing authentic and when is it simply proving?

It has been in the waiting that I've learned to tell the difference.

There is nothing wrong with being someone who strives, delights in learning and creating, and finds joy in activity and achievement. But when we never pause to wait, the efforting becomes the weight.

That is why I value Mark Nepo's reminder. He is a gentle, reflective soul, yet even he admits to a life once driven by achievement and the need to prove himself to people who didn't deserve a seat at his table. For him, it took cancer, twice, to awaken.

As I continue to untuck myself, I realize the practice is less about abandoning one way of being and more about shifting between effort and stillness. Some days I need solitude; others, I need action. The balance keeps me centered. The energy behind it is what matters most.

Whisper:

Thank you, God, for the beauty of this morning and for this stillness with You. Here, I gather in Your grace. Here, I remember I am enough. Bring me back to this place each day, where I can simply BE.

Prompt:

What does waiting feel like for you right now?
How could God be meeting you in the wait?

Positive Solitude

Reflection:

There is a difference between retreating out of exhaustion and retreating out of love. In the early days of craving solitude, I was simply desperate to escape the noise, the demands, and the constant tug of other people's needs. But as time went on, I discovered something deeper: the gift of chosen solitude. Psychologists call this "positive solitude," the kind of being alone that nourishes rather than isolates, heals rather than hardens.

In positive solitude, my own company suffices. I notice that the more I learn to sit with myself, the more discerning I become about who and what I allow into my space. It isn't avoidance. Its alignment. The quiet reveals what truly feeds my spirit and what drains it.

This kind of solitude doesn't isolate me from the world; it grounds me in a way that makes connections more genuine. When I emerge from this inward space, I do so with clarity rather than exhaustion. Positive solitude is where I learn to reconnect with myself, not out of loneliness but out of love.

Whisper:

Holy Spirit

Quiet my mind

Let my breath and spirit align

So that I am present in this place and time

Help me to ease anxieties that keep me from my peace

To trust in you and come from a place of gratitude

So that I can shine my light and all that is Divine inside

Prompt:

What steps can you take today to generate positive solitude
for yourself?

GJP: Gratitude, Joy, Peace

Reflection:

I've always loved a good acronym—LOL, WTF, IYKYK. And my personal favorite, GJP. A powerful acronym to anchor me every day. GJP = Gratitude, Joy, Peace.

These three words have become part of my daily prayers and inner compass. Each day, I pause and ask: What has brought me gratitude, joy, and peace today?

A good day grounds me in appreciation.

When the day is hard, it redirects my focus from what's wrong to what's still right.

Sometimes I even sing it in my head, a silly little tune, the kind Phoebe from Friends might come up with while shampooing her hair.

Lather, rinse, repeat.

Lather, rinse, repeat.

GJP, GJP, GJP… as needed.

IYKYK

It makes me smile every time. A small, sacred ritual disguised as humor, but one that realigns my heart with gratitude, joy, and peace.

Whisper:

"Gratitude turns what we have into enough." —Anonymous

Prompt:

What three words would guide your day if you let them? Write them down. Then, at the end of today, ask yourself how they appeared in small or big ways.

This Is the Day

Reflection:

"This is the day the Lord has made; let us rejoice and be glad in it."—Psalm 118:24

You've probably heard the verse. Maybe even sung it in church. But how often do we actually live it, especially on the days that don't go as planned?

Some mornings we wake up with purpose, ready to have a good day. Then: the coffee maker breaks, the Wi-Fi drops, traffic jams or someone nearby releases their bad mood into our space. Suddenly, our happiness is hijacked.

This happened to me during a season when I was already carrying too much. I'd been pushing hard, doing everything "right," but still felt the heavy ache of pressure and expectation. One quiet morning, just as I'd settled into a moment of calm, something small but sharp disrupted it, a miscommunication. The kind of conflict that shouldn't rattle your soul, but somehow it does. The other person moved on. But I didn't. Their frustration clung to me, adding to the weight I was already carrying.

I stepped outside to catch my breath, and there, perched in a nearby tree, was a bright red cardinal. Immediately, the verse flooded my spirit:

This is the day the Lord has made...

My body relaxed. Not because the tension disappeared, but because I was reminded of what truly matters.

God chose to wake me up that day. And like every day, that day was a gift.

We have the power to choose how we live in each moment, including the messy ones.

Peace doesn't come from avoiding irritations; it comes from choosing who we are despite them.

Whisper:

Holy Spirit, guide me back to the truth when I feel frustrated. Help me face each day with gratitude, not just when it's easy, but especially when it's hard.

Prompt:

How often do you let small irritations ruin your energy for the day?

What would it be like to rejoice and be glad, even when things don't go as planned?

The Space In Between

Reflection:

When the noise quiets and the roles we've played begin to unravel, we're left with... space. It can feel like a void at first, a silence so loud it's almost uncomfortable. But when I finally allowed myself to rest, to stop performing, I realized the pause wasn't empty at all.

My intermission wasn't just a break; it was a becoming. It was the slow exhale after years of holding my breath. In the quiet, I could finally hear myself again. Not the echo of expectations or the static of self-doubt, but the authentic voice beneath it all, the one that had been waiting patiently.

During that pause, I reevaluated everything: what I valued, what I tolerated, what I believed. I mourned what I had outgrown. I loosened my grip on identities that were never truly mine. As I shed the layers, I started to hear God more clearly.

Sometimes, the most sacred work occurs not in doing, but in undoing. In surrender. In the intermission.

If you find yourself in that space, in the not yet, the in-between, don't rush through it. Don't fill it just to avoid the discomfort. Stay a while. Listen. Trust that something holy is unfolding, even if you can't see it yet.

Whisper:

Even my pauses serve a purpose.

Prompt:

Have you ever resisted rest, only to find it was where your healing began?

Section I

Stillness Speaks

In Closing:

A Blessing for Stillness

May the tranquility you've found in these pages ground you when the world pulls you away.

May you come to trust the wisdom within you.

May the pause become a practice.

A place you return to, again and again, to remember who you are.

And when you're ready, may stillness softly guide you toward your next brave transformation.

Section II

The Courage to Rise

"The journey to happiness involves finding the courage to go down into ourselves and take responsibility for what's there: all of it." —Richard Rohr

There comes a moment on every healing journey when the soul begins to stir, whispering: It's time.

Rising up to that inner stir takes great courage, not because of doubt, but because you finally stop waiting for permission.

It involves listening to the wisdom of your inner mentor, speaking the truth even when your voice trembles, and learning to hold both your tenderness and power simultaneously.

It takes courage to look inward and accept responsibility.

These reflections are for those times when you want to fall back asleep and a deeper part of you refuses to let you.

You are free to rise slowly. Unapologetically. Authentically.

This courage grows from the stillness you've started to nurture. It supports you when you're alone and lifts your SELF to the next level.

Much of this part of the journey, you will continue to do alone behind the scenes. You'll find a few sacred hearts that will hold space for you, but ultimately the work is yours to do.

You will need to let go of anger, fear, worry, shame, resentment, pity… Need I go on?

I pray these words will be a blessing to you when you feel like no one understands. You are not alone! I promise.

Tapestry Unfolding

Reflection:

A Tapestry Unfolding – A Poem

What has life sewn in you?

Wrinkles of worry,

Spots of time,

Crevices of courage,

Lines of love and laughter.

Threads of life intertwined.

They hold your strength,

They tell your story.

Patches that weave together

The fabric of you,

Some pristine and delicate,

Some worn and torn

Yet all come together.

No need for perfection, my sweet girl.

Your tapestry is layered with love,

Stories of heartbreak

Survival and wisdom,

Grace and humility.
A beautiful tapestry
A life lived and still unfolding.

There will be a moment when your life encourages you to unfold. You will realize that every scar holds a thread of truth: the seasons you pushed yourself far beyond what you believed you could handle.

Today, I choose to see myself not as a project to be fixed but as a tapestry still unfolding. Some parts are soft and new, some patched from things I thought might break me. Some worn from love and use. And still, I am here. Still unfolding. Still loved.

Whisper:

Breathe in: *I honor my unfolding.*
Breathe out: *I release the need to hide.*

Prompt:

What thread, grief, grace, joy, or courage wants to be named and honored today?
Can you face it with compassion as your tapestry unfolds?

The Quiet Grip of Resistance

Reflection:

"Change is never painful. Only the resistance to change is painful." —Buddha

Resistance is sneaky. It slips into our thoughts and disguises itself as protection, whispering that staying safe and unseen is the wisest choice. It knows our fears by heart and keeps track of our deepest insecurities. Its promise is comfort, but that comfort comes at a price.

For years, I moved through life with resistance quietly clinging to my steps. In my career, I was confident and capable, but in my personal life, fear of the unknown kept me paralyzed. I mistook familiarity for safety, even when it left me unfulfilled. That was the cruel trick of resistance: it made my prison feel like home.

It wasn't until a moment of intense shaking that I realized how much of my life I was resisting. The truth is that resistance only has power when we allow it to take hold.

The moment we take even the smallest step forward, its hold starts to loosen.

That first step is never easy. It can feel like entering the wilderness without a map. But comfort was never the goal. Growth happens in the tension. Courage is born in the unknown. And each time we face resistance, we get closer to the life God planned for us.

If resistance whispers in your ear, I encourage you to respond with action, no matter how small or imperfect. Remember: you were not made to stay hidden. You have gifts, passions and purpose. Every step you take beyond fear is a step toward your truest self.

Whisper:

God, grant me the courage to confront the places where I feel stuck. Remind me that You did not create me to live in fear, but to embrace the gifts You have given me fully. When resistance whispers, help me to respond with faith and action.

Prompt:

Where in your life do you feel resistance keeping you "safe," and how might taking one small step forward loosen its grip?

Cutting the Strings: Then and Now

Reflection:

Then – 2016:

"Anything or anyone that asks you to be other than yourself is not Holy but is trying only to fill its own need."
—Mark Nepo

When I first read that quote, it moved me enough to write about it in 2016. At the time, it felt very familiar to me.

I realize how profoundly I was shaped by the need to please others, to fit in, and avoid conflict. I didn't just tuck my fringe; I stitched it down. I played the puppet. I allowed others to mold and silence me, even as something inside longed to break free.

And still, my journal read:

Though it's hard to break free from my puppeteers' strings, living my truth feels so much more liberating. Scary sometimes, but worth it.

I was starting to realize that my tendency to give wasn't the issue. The real problem was forgetting that I was also worthy of receiving. I didn't owe my peace to anyone's comfort.

Now – 2025:

I see how true those words are today and how far I've come. I no longer confuse love with appeasement. I no longer call it loyalty when I abandon myself.

My "fringe" is no longer something I need to hide; it's a sacred expression of who I am.

I've learned that untucking isn't a one-time act. It's a daily devotion. Some days, I still catch myself slipping back into old roles. But now, I recognize the pattern. I hear the whisper of my own voice returning. I remember:

I'm not here to be who others need me to be.

I am here to be who I was divinely created to be.

Whisper:

Let me remember, God, that I am not too much, too confident, too sensitive. Let me stand in my truth with grace and let those who love me meet me there.

Prompt:

What roles or expectations have you had to let go of to stay true to yourself?

What has "untucking your fringe" meant for you over the past decade?

One Step Forward

Reflection:

God, I know I tend to try to have everything figured out, but this I don't. I just can't. I know ultimately You are in charge, but I pray now for You to cover me with courage. I don't know how to pick my SELF up and walk out that door. I don't know how to take the first step to save my SELF. I know it will be hard. But I also know that if I stay, I will slowly die from the inside out. I can already feel it happening and I know You created me for more. Please give me the courage I need to take this first step. (Journal entry June 17, 2019)

There are moments in life when you know deep in your bones that staying would mean slowly disappearing. Not physically, but soulfully.

And yet, leaving seems impossible. Not because the path is unclear, but because your legs have forgotten how to walk toward your own being.

This is the ache of thresholds, that quiet moment when you whisper:

"I can't stay, but I don't yet know how to go."

I once sat with this ache, curled up on the floor, unsure whether my prayer would reach beyond the ceiling. I didn't ask for a miracle. I didn't ask for everything to be fixed. I just asked for enough courage to take one single step.

And that's where God met me.

Not with fireworks or easy answers, but with a gentle blanket of courage that wrapped me and whispered, 'Just take the first step.' The step was mine, but the strength? It came from somewhere greater.

Whisper:

"But he said to me, 'My grace is sufficient for you, for my power is made perfect in weakness.'

Therefore I will boast all the more gladly about my weaknesses, so that Christ's power may rest on me." 2 Corinthians 12:9 (NIV)

Prompt:

Is there a door your soul knows it needs to walk through, but fear has kept you paralyzed?

What if you asked for the courage to take one step instead of all at once?

Gradually, God Said

Reflection:

"If the goal doesn't fit with My will for you, I will **gradually** change the desire of your heart."
— March 8 Devotional, *Jesus Calling*

I highlighted those words in March 2018 without realizing how deeply they would influence the year ahead. Twelve months later, I read them again, and they resonated with greater clarity.

It's a single word that speaks the loudest: gradually.

I've never been good with gradual change. I prefer clear timelines and measurable goals. But nothing about healing is linear. There's no "done" stamp when you're untucking from a life of people-pleasing and perfectionism.

My untucking started at the top of Cathedral Rock in Sedona in 2018. The wind swirled, time seemed to stand still, and I descended the red rock trail, thinking I'd let go of everything by the time I reached the bottom. But it never happens in just one moment.

God wasn't asking me to purge my pain in just one

hike. He was asking me to surrender my timeline.

What followed was a season of shedding beliefs, relationships, routines, and expectations. It was disorienting yet beautiful. I found myself in self-uncovery, laying down every tool and hustle, waiting to see what was truly mine to carry.

The process of untucking is seldom loud. It is a whisper. A redirection. A return.

Whisper:

Change me gradually, God. When I seek quick answers, guide me back to trust. I release the timeline and only ask to be aligned with You.

Prompt:

Where in your life have you hoped for quick change but been led on a slow path?

What does *self-uncovery* look like for you right now, and can you honor its pace?

Half Butterfly

Reflection:

"To everything there is a season, and a time to every purpose under the heaven… A time to break down, and a time to build up." —Ecclesiastes 3:1,3

Living this life, I worked so hard to create after healing the big wounds and learning how to love my SELF, it feels lonelier than I expected.

Boundaries, once nonexistent, are now so defined they almost feel like barricades. I wonder sometimes if I've swung too far to the other side. From doormat to fortress. From too accommodating to unapproachable. Like the old neighbor yelling, "Get off my lawn!"

I ask myself, is there a part of me I'm still afraid to touch?

Am I hiding behind these ironclad boundaries to avoid the risk of rejection?

It feels as if I'm half-born.

Half a butterfly, with the remnants of the caterpillar still clinging to me, weighing me down.

What does it feel like to be in the center? When was the last time I felt both terrified and free?

I think back to that day.

The day I left, I had nowhere to go.

Staying on borrowed couches.

Surrounded by fear and yet, for the first time in years, breathing freedom.

The knowing: *I cannot go back.*

That's when I started to trust the unfolding.

That's when I stopped asking for permission to live my truth.

Now I wonder, how can I return to that inner place, not the fear, but the courage?

How do I soften these walls without losing my SELF again?

Maybe it's not about swinging the pendulum.

Maybe it's about learning how to hover near the center, where boundaries are grounded in love, not defense.

Whisper:

I trust the gradual, imperfect unfolding. I am learning to live with my wings fully open.

Prompt:

Where might you be overprotecting yourself out of fear rather than love?

What does your version of "center" look and feel like today?

Healing the Girl Within

Reflection:

"The child is still there. If you're not in touch with that child, you're not in touch with the deepest part of yourself." —Thich Nhat Hanh

She's still in there, the girl with scraped knees and a big heart. The one who giggled freely but also learned to stay quiet to be liked. The girl who twirled in the yard with bare feet and big feelings, then shrank to survive.

She learned early how to please others, how to smile and nod, how to carry the weight of others' comfort in her tiny hands. She tucked her fringe to fit in but never stopped hoping someone would see her and say, "You don't have to earn your worth."

That someone turned out to be me.

When I stopped trying to fix her and began listening, something sacred occurred. I realized she didn't need to be saved; she just needed to be loved and to hear it spoken to her.

I see you. You matter. I am here now.

Untucking isn't about rewriting the past; it's about becoming the person your younger self needed. That girl inside doesn't need your shame. She needs your presence. She needs you to make different choices today, choices that honor her voice, her wonder, and her wholeness.

Whisper:

Find a photo of yourself as a child. Sit with it. Gaze softly into her eyes.

I'm really proud of you. I'm sorry you felt lonely. I promise I will never leave you again.

Prompt:

What does your inner child need from you today?

How can you give her joy, protection, and softness right now?

Inside Voices

Reflection:

Death and life are in the power of the tongue."

—Proverbs 18:21

For years, I lived with that voice whispering:

You're too sensitive.

You should've known better.

You're not good enough

Shame on you

It's strange how loud those voices get when we're silent. They are echoes of survival, old stories we had to believe to stay in our place.

But they are not the truth.

The truth is softer. Kinder. She sounds like mercy, like breath, like love.

Start to observe the voice inside. Is it soft or harsh? Does it support or tear down?

If a friend talked to you the way you speak to yourself, would you feel safe?

Sometimes, healing starts not by silencing the inner

critic, but by saying:

I hear you. I understand you were trying to protect me. But I don't need you to run the show anymore.

Whisper:

May I become fluent in the language of compassion and speak to myself as someone worth loving.

Prompt:

Close your eyes and take a deep breath. Bring to mind a time when you were hard on yourself.

Now ask:

Whose voice does this resemble?

What did I need at that moment instead?

Can I show that kindness to myself now?

Even a single moment of compassion starts to reprogram the brain to choose love instead of fear.

Awakening Through the Dark Night

Reflection:

In a moment of quiet reflection, I find myself thinking about the dark night of the soul. As I watch the subtle shift between darkness and dawn, I realize that life may be a series of dark nights, each one challenging us and leading us into a deeper, more authentic version of ourselves. Crisis becomes the gateway through which we heal and transform.

There is something sacred about how a crisis strips us bare. It brings us to a place of such vulnerability that the old ways of controlling and protecting ourselves simply fall apart. In that untucking, we surrender. We allow the deeper powers of our soul and the Divine to slip in through the cracks we never meant to expose. Without crisis, we rarely step out of the comfortable patterns that keep us small, even when those patterns have become a crisis of their own.

I see now the lens I once lived behind, the blinders I clung to, and the ways I refused to see the truth because truth demanded change. But once you wake up and feel the truth of who you are, you can't tuck yourself back into numbness.

For so long, I lived in chaos and the consuming turbulence of absorbing another person's unhealed pain. Now, away from all that, I can finally hear myself again. And what I hear is that I don't want to survive anymore. I want to live.

And to live, I need space. I need truth. I need nature. I need God.

Looking back, I see how crisis shaped me. How darkness became a catalyst. How every night that felt like it might swallow me whole ended up becoming part of my rising. Every unraveling made room. Every surrender strengthened my connection to the Divine.

It isn't lost on me how small I am in this vast universe. Yet somehow, I feel more connected, more awake, more alive in God than I ever have before. Maybe that's what the dark night teaches us. Not how to avoid the darkness, but how to let it remake us into someone who can carry the light.

Whisper:

"The dark night of the soul is a journey into light, a journey from your darkness into the strength and hidden resources of your soul." —Caroline Myss

Prompt:

What crisis in your life transformed you more than it broke you?

What did it awaken in you that comfort never could?

Letter To My Becoming

Reflection:

Dearest heart, you are extraordinary.

As you continue your journey, you discover more of who God made you to be. Worthy in creation, perfectly imperfect. No one else's approval is needed.

You've released the need to chase after affection and attention, and in doing so, you've discovered freedom. It's not a freedom you had to earn, but one that has always been yours.

The freedom to be yourself.

And that freedom? It's weightless.

So... who are you becoming?

I love my mind, body, and heart.

I wake up excited to create the day. What a gift! A walk helps me adjust to an awakened state. My morning ritual brings peace and aligns me with what God has in store.

Exercise is no longer punishment; it's play.

Healthy food is no longer control; it's nourishment.

Learning and working keep me vibrant and alive.

I'm surrounded by beauty and things that bring me joy.
I am proud and excited to live life fully.
God validates me.
I validate me.
Love,
ME

Whisper:

My freedom was never external; it has always been within, waiting to be remembered.

Prompt:

If you wrote a letter to your heart today, what would you say to affirm the becoming already in motion within you?

More Than Enough

Reflection:

"I AM WHO I AM."—Exodus 3:14

The phrase "you are enough" echoes everywhere these days. It's written in affirmations, stitched into pillows, and spoken like gospel to our tired, trying hearts.

At first, I clung to it.

I needed it.

Years ago, saying "I am enough" felt like defiance, an anthem for the part of me that had hustled and overextended just to feel worthy.

But eventually, something about it didn't sit right.

Enough started to feel like a ceiling rather than a foundation.

A compromise instead of a celebration.

Enough… by whose standards?

If I am created in the image of God, formed from love, purpose, and breath, then why would I settle for enough?

Why wouldn't I dare to live fully, freely, and abundantly?

God didn't create me to be almost enough. He called His creation very good.

That's more than enough. That's extraordinary.

And here's what I've come to understand:

"I am enough" may be where the healing begins, but it's not where the soul stops.

When I live aligned with God, I live from a place beyond measurement, beyond comparison, beyond chasing.

Because I am.

And that's the sacred truth.

"I AM," said God to Moses in the wilderness.

Not *I am trying.*

Not *I am almost.*

Just: **I AM.**

Eternal. Whole. Already complete.

And we are created in that image.

So I'm learning to lay down enough like the armor it has become.

To stop auditioning.

To remember who I am, including my gifts and flaws, my courage and softness, is enough.

Whisper:

I am not here to be enough. I am here to be complete.

Prompt:

What does "enough" mean to you today?

Where might you be called to go beyond it? To live from abundance rather than constant striving?

The Critics

Reflection:

"It is not the critic who counts... The credit belongs to the one who is actually in the arena..." —Theodore Roosevelt

The first time I read this quote, I was in my mid-forties. It moved me so much that I ordered a framed version for my wall, and it still hangs in my office.

Over the years, my admiration for these words has evolved. Initially, they felt like a rallying cry for the overachiever in me; the one who always felt she didn't measure up. Roosevelt's words gave me the confidence to confront certain people and assert myself both verbally and mentally.

But now, when I pause to read them (and I do this often), they hit differently.

I've been my own harshest critic, even though I didn't want to admit it for a long time. Every criticism or judgment I received, I accepted as truth. Instead of seeing that most criticism is just a reflection of someone else's insecurity, I took it as marching orders: work harder, do more, prove yourself.

What I realize now is that the harshest criticism often came from people who were supposed to love me. That made me chase their approval even more, feeding my inner critic until it became louder than my own truth. The reality is, some people will always have something to say about anyone and everything. And that leaves me with a choice: keep wasting my energy, time, and peace on their opinions or let them move on to their next target while I stay grounded in who I really am.

Brené Brown calls this kind of criticism the "cheap seats." The people who sit high up in the arena, never daring to step onto the floor themselves, are always the first to deliver insults and criticism. From a distance, it feels safe to tear others down. But as Brené says, "If you're not in the arena getting your ass kicked, I'm not interested in your opinion or feedback."

That doesn't mean we don't care. Of course, we do; we're human, and words can hurt. But the key difference is this: we don't have to let those opinions define us or remove us from the game.

If you're in the arena, daring, rising, even failing, you're already ahead of those who never risk showing up. And that is what truly matters.

Whisper:

The cheap seats don't get to control the story I tell with my life.

Prompt:

Whose opinions have you been clinging to that aren't really yours?

What would happen if you stopped listening to their voices and trusted your own instead?

No Stone Left Unturned

Reflection:

"And the day came when the risk to remain tight in a bud was more painful than the risk it took to blossom."
—*Anaïs Nin*

How can you tell when you've healed enough to move on?

I've turned over every stone, shadow, and thread and traced every wound back to its root.

I've cried tears, screamed screams, written the letters I'll never send.

And still I ask:

Have I done enough?

Is there one more thing to uncover?

Or am I just delaying the moment when I must trust myself to live?

It's strange how easy it is to stay in the comfort of the work.

Because the work is familiar. It gives me purpose. It protects me from risk.

But healing can also become a hiding place.

And I wonder:

Am I afraid of slipping back into old patterns, or am I afraid of being fully seen and possibly rejected?

What does it feel like to be completely safe in my body?

What does peace feel like in a relationship, genuine, consistent, uneventful peace?

This season of my life urges me not to dig deeper, but to root myself more firmly. To trust that the healing I've done is enough.

To believe that I can take all I've learned and live it, rather than constantly analyzing everything.

Whisper:

I trust what I've uncovered. I am prepared to live from what I've reclaimed.

Prompt:

Where in your life are you still "doing the work" when it might be time to just live?

What might it feel like to stop uncovering and start embodying?

The Battle I Didn't Know I Was Fighting

Reflection:

There are many types of battles.

Some explode loudly and quickly, others last for decades, fought in whispers no one else can hear.

The quiet battle is the hardest to name, the one fought inside your own skin. It's the battle where you lose pieces of yourself one polite smile at a time, one apology you didn't owe, one compromise too many.

For years, I stayed where I wasn't truly seen, where I was diminished into someone smaller, softer, easier to control. And for years, I justified it. I called it patience.

Loyalty.

Resilience.

It's easy to confuse endurance with love, especially for those of us who were taught early on that being "good" meant being quiet and agreeable.

But love never requires silencing your soul.

And peace? It's not the absence of conflict; it's the presence of truth.

Looking back, I see how I used kindness as a shield. I tended to over function, apologize excessively, and over-perform because I feared that if I stopped, I'd be unlovable.

And the quiet battle ended the day I stopped waging it against myself.

Whisper:

May I no longer confuse silence with strength.

May I remember that my voice, my truth, and my worth are sacred.

May I learn to stand in love, and may every quiet war I've fought lead me home.

Prompt:

Where in your life have you stayed quiet or played small to keep the peace?

What could it look like to make peace with yourself instead?

Truth I Will Not Tuck

Reflection:

"You will become a graveyard of all the women you once were. Before you rise one morning embraced by your own skin You will swallow a thousand different names before you taste the meaning held within your own." —Pavana Reddy

"I live my truth and do not tuck my fringe for anyone."

This line, the second in a prayer I wrote in 2016, has become a compass for my life.

Every morning, I recite it. Every night, I'm prompted to reflect on where I might have hidden parts of myself again out of fear, habit, or comfort.

Living my truth isn't polished. It's messy. But it's sacred.

It means embracing everything. It means reclaiming what I've spent years trying to suppress because it didn't fit.

And when I started asking better questions:

Why do I ignore my needs to protect someone else's peace?

Why do I carry shame for being too much and not enough?

Why do I stay where I am, slowly fading away?

The answers unraveled me because I wasn't just hiding from the world; I was hiding from myself.

Truth-telling is a daily practice. It means holding space for beauty and regret, grief and growth.

It means saying, "Yes, that really happened."

And then choosing not to define yourself by that pain, but by what you've chosen since.

My truth isn't tidy. But it's mine.

It's sexy because it's real.

So, no.

I won't tuck my fringe.

Not for approval.

Not for comfort.

Not even for love.

This life is mine to live, and I'm showing up with all of myself.

Whisper:

My truth doesn't have to be palatable to be powerful.

Prompt:

Where are you still tucking your truth to keep others comfortable?

What part of you is ready to emerge, even if it's messy and misunderstood?

The Gentle Art of Forgiveness

Reflection:

Forgive and you will be forgiven. —Luke 6:37

There comes a time when the heart can no longer bear the weight of old wounds.

The stories. The grudges. The shame.

The moments we wish we could undo on both sides of the mirror.

This prayer is not a formula.

It is a softening. A sacred invitation to connect with ourselves and others through our shared humanity.

Let these words serve as your prayer today. Whisper them softly:

Buddhist Forgiveness Prayer

If I have harmed anyone in any way,
either knowingly or unknowingly,
through my own confusion

I ask their forgiveness.
If anyone has harmed me in any way,
either knowingly or unknowingly,
through their own confusion
I forgive them.
And if there is a situation I am not yet ready to forgive,
I forgive myself for that.
For all the ways I harm myself
negate, doubt, belittle, judge,
or treat myself unkindly through my own confusion
I forgive myself.

Whisper:

Forgiveness isn't always a moment.
Sometimes, it's a slow, gentle process, like untangling the knots
we've tied around our hearts.
Let this practice be enough for today.
Let it begin with compassion.
Let it begin with you.

Prompt:

Where in your life are you being called to soften the edges
of your heart?
Is there someone, even yourself, you are ready to start for-
giving, in your own time, in your own way?

Will I Ever Learn

Reflection:

There are times when the pain comes back unexpectedly, when I feel the sting of old patterns and wonder if I've truly grown at all.

My heart aches again.

And in that pain, a familiar thought comes back: Maybe it's me.

But another voice, quieter but stronger, reminds me:

I have learned so much.

I've begun to truly see myself, the daughter God created.

I've started standing up for her. Letting her speak. Letting her feel.

Letting her be seen.

And yet, each time I get up, I feel a sting of disappointment.

I notice the subtle ways others once benefited from my silence, from my bending.

I see how I tried to meet their expectations, keep the peace, and earn their love, even at the expense of my own soul.

I didn't want to believe it, but I do now: some people loved me more when I didn't love myself.

And perhaps the most heartbreaking truth of all:

I let it happen.

I abandoned myself just to be accepted.

That realization hurts, but it also heals.

Because self-awareness is the first step toward freedom.

Not all at once. Not perfectly.

But with each return to myself, I claim a little more light.

Maybe healing isn't about finishing the lesson.

Maybe it's about showing up again and again with compassion each time I'm tempted to forget.

Whisper:

Holy Spirit, stay close as I work through these old patterns. Help me feel what I once denied and grieve what I once accepted. Show me what freedom looks like from the inside out. Let this awareness become a doorway, not a prison.

Prompt:

What does "not abandoning yourself" look like today?

The Ache Between Surrender and Trust

Reflection:

I thought I had clarity after my pilgrimage.

I believed my energy would return, my body would be rested, and the peace I felt on the path would stay with me at home.

But instead, I arrived home dizzy, sleep-deprived, emotional, and wobbly in more ways than one.

And one night, after Mass, everything I had been holding in finally cracked open.

It poured out of me, not as a prayer or poem, but as a rant.

A holy, tired, soul-weary rant.

I'm tired of healing.

Tired of pretending the waiting doesn't hurt.

Tired of being told that "it will all make sense someday."

I have done the work.

I've realigned, released, surrendered, and trusted.

I've said no to old patterns.

I've chosen peace over people-pleasing.

And yet, here I am, wondering if I'm being punished or protected.

Then I remember…

What I do have is a heart that's still soft, a soul still listening, and a willingness to speak even when it isn't pretty.

Maybe you've been here too.

Maybe you're here now.

And if so, I want you to know your truth belongs here as well. You don't need to spiritualize, reframe, or fix it. Even the fatigue, the longing, the ache is part of the untucking.

The holy unraveling of hidden places.

Whisper:

I can be tired and faithful. I can be uncertain and still in the process of unfolding.

Prompt:

What truth are you keeping to yourself because it still doesn't feel "wrapped in hope" yet?

Meeting the Inner Mentor

Reflection:

"Before I formed you in the womb, I knew you."
—Jeremiah 1:5

A part of me has always known her. She emerges in stillness. In an image of my older self, standing in her garden at her lake cottage, gray hair and a gentle smile rising like mist from a life well lived. She remains grounded, content, knowing.

She is my inner mentor, the version of me who has already survived heartbreaks, forgiven mistakes, and found peace in her skin.

For decades, I kept returning to her. In moments of doubt, I would close my eyes and picture her standing there, whispering:

You already know the way.

We all carry this future self within us. A voice not molded by fear or trauma, but by wisdom and alignment. She is not a fantasy; she is a blueprint.

What if your wisest self is already present, not just at

the end of your journey, but deep within you today? What if she's been waiting for you to listen?

Let her speak and guide you toward choices that honor your wholeness.

Whisper:

May I remember that wisdom lives within me.
May I trust the quiet voice that already knows.
May I walk each step with the woman I am becoming.

Prompt:

Find a quiet space and close your eyes.

Visualize your older, wiser self, maybe 10, 20, or 30 years from now.

Notice:

What does she look like?

Where is she?

How does she spend her days?

What does she want you to know?

Ask her one question that's been on your mind. Trust her response.

What Are You Willing to Risk to Untuck Yourself?

Reflection:

One morning, I asked myself a question in my journal: *What have I risked to live in my truth?*

At first, I wasn't sure how to answer.

But as I sat with the question a little longer, I realized it feels like I've risked everything.

Vulnerability.

Isolation.

Misunderstanding.

Loss of friends. Family. Familiarity.

Loss of the life I knew how to hold.

Loss of the life that once held me.

But when I look at that list now, I can see how temporary those losses were.

They stripped me down, yes

but they also upgraded me.

In releasing what wasn't truly mine, I made room for

something far more sacred:

clarity, freedom, and the quiet strength of becoming who I actually am.

For years, I stayed stuck in the lies I told myself:

that I was fine,

that I could endure anything,

that this was simply how life was supposed to feel.

Those lies were a kind of safety.

A soft blanket that kept me warm

even as it kept me small.

It's astonishing how long we can live inside our own stories.

Stories that keep the peace for everyone except the person living them.

Stories that protect us from the unknown,

even while they suffocate the very truth that wants to rise.

Safety is not the same as peace.

Pretending is not the same as living.

When we finally dare to tell ourselves the truth

even when it unravels the life we worked so hard to maintain

we open the door to everything that is real.

The truth will cost you your illusions.

But it will give you yourself in return.

So I ask you, gently and honestly:

What are you willing to risk to untuck your truth?

What comfort, story, expectation, or identity

might you be asked to loosen your grip on

so that your soul can breathe?

You may not know what is on the other side of letting

go.

I didn't either.

But years later, I can tell you

the risk was the bridge to the life I was meant to live.

Whisper:

"Until you make the unconscious conscious, it will direct your life, and you will call it fate." —Carl Jung

Prompt:

What truth about your life have you been afraid to admit to yourself, and what might your life open into if you dared to name it?

Longing to Become — A Meditation

Reflection:

There are moments when truth rises from somewhere deep within.

It happens in the ordinary
As you slip into your slippers in the early morning.
It comes as a random thought, soft but unmistakable:
What an extraordinary life we are given, if we choose to open ourselves to it.
Gratitude wells up.
Not just for family, home, and health,
but for the invitation to live honestly.
To live untucked.
To stop hiding the parts of our essence we once folded away
to be accepted, loved, or safe.
This honest opening is holy work,
and the Trinity meets us there.

There is the One who Creates
the Source who imagined your wholeness
long before you were taught to shrink.
There is the One who Walks With
the Companion beside you
when the truth feels heavy or disruptive.
There is the One who Dwells Within
the inner stirring that refuses to let you forget
who you really are.
The Trinity holds a piece of your becoming.
The Father whispers possibility.
The Son offers courage.
The Holy Spirit awakens longing.
Yet even in gratitude, something stirs.
A life that looks good on the outside, even blessed,
and still something essential remains hidden.
Something longed for.
Something true.
The realization that you've tucked away your essence
can be painful.
Not because your life is bad,
but because you sense the cost
of living smaller than the soul you were given.
You can numb this knowing with distractions, ambitions, roles or habits…
but it always returns.
A gentle insistence.

A holy nudge.
A call to step forward in truth.
The Trinity holds you as you ask yourself:
What part of me is still tucked away?
What am I afraid will happen if I let it be seen?
What would my life look like if I allowed that truth to emerge?

Whisper:

Breathe deeply.
Place a hand on your heart if you'd like.
Feel the warmth of your own presence,
your own existence.
You are not alone in this becoming.
You never have been.
The Father delights in your unfolding.
The Son walks beside your trembling steps.
The Holy Spirit within whispers,
This longing is not your enemy; it is your guide.

Prompt:

What is one thing I am ready to untuck today?
Even the smallest untucking is sacred.
Even the slightest act of truth-telling
can change the shape of your life.
You are held in the mystery.
You are guided in the becoming.

You are free to live the fullness of who you are
no longer tucked.
You are allowed to grow.
You are allowed to rise.
You are allowed to live untucked.

Walking Through the Threshold

Reflection:

"We do not think ourselves into new ways of living. We live ourselves into new ways of thinking." —Richard Rohr
Journey to the Center

When you recognize yourself as the treasure you truly are, you can no longer settle for the safety of living small. To step into your own light, you must be willing to confront everything that stands between you and your inner divinity.

Once you cross that threshold, there's no turning back.

To retreat would be the greatest act of violence against your spirit.

So why do we stay where we know we don't belong?

Fear of the unknown.

Fear of what's on the other side.

Crossing the threshold changes everything. You can no longer revisit the pain or keep telling the old story. You can't use it as your identity or your fuel. It's still a part of you, but it no longer defines you.

And that's why it's so difficult. You're not just facing the unknown; you're also letting go of the familiar story you've told yourself for years.

Who am I without it?

It kept you stuck, but it also kept you safe. It made you feel like you were making progress, but you were always one step forward, two steps back, or stuck on the fence, staring at the grass on both sides.

The truth is, once you step through, you find solid ground beneath your feet, and it's greener than you've ever imagined.

Whisper:

As I step forward with courage, my story isn't over; it's just the beginning.

Prompt:

What feels like your threshold right now? What fear or pattern might be holding you back from stepping forward? What would it look like to live from the place on the other side of that threshold?

Section II

The Courage to Rise

In Closing:

A Blessing for Courage

May this be the turning point, the moment you stop apologizing for who you are becoming.

The moment your truth no longer waits for permission.

The moment you remember: untucking is not a phase, it is the way forward.

As you rise,

May you feel the ground steady beneath your feet,

And the Sacred stirring within your chest.

May your truth become a torch,

Lighting the path not only for you but also for those who are still afraid to speak.

A beacon

You are ready to belong

To your voice,
To your life,
To your Self.

Section III

Sacred Belonging

Sacred belonging is the deep exhale that follows courage. It is the place you arrive at after rising, where striving eases, and the heart finally rests in the truth of who you are.

Here, belonging is no longer something you have to chase outside of yourself. It is a sacred coming home within. It is where you reconnect with God through Love. It is where grace welcomes you in the ordinary rhythms of your life.

Sacred belonging is the understanding that you are always held, that nothing can separate you from the Love that created you. It is the foundation where peace, trust, and authenticity thrive.

This is where we stop asking, "Do I belong?" and start living as if we already do.

Yellow Curtains

Reflection:

"Truly I tell you, unless you change and become like little children, you will never enter the kingdom of heaven."
—Matthew 18:3

Yellow Curtains - A Poem

What was my first thought?
I wish I could remember.
My first memory: a room with yellow curtains,
sunlight spilling like honey across the dark wood floor.
A child-sized table and two tiny chairs wait for a tea party
with stuffed friends.
In that room, I was simply my truest self,
full of joy,
full of curiosity,
full of potential.
No thoughts carefully curated.
No insecurities hidden.
Nothing to change or become.

But somewhere
a whisper became a thought,
a thought became a rule,
a rule became a wall.
And so I started building
my house of thoughts,
layered with wallpapered beliefs,
A cheerful facade covering the hairline cracks underneath.
Hung curtain after curtain
stitched with expectation
to soften the harsh edges,
shade my joy,
cover my truth.
But the walls remember.
The cracks widened beneath my silence.
The rooms darkened with time.
The cheerful colors faded.
How do I save this home I've lived in for so long
that once held sunlight and sweetness?
Can I peel back the faded wallpaper and uncover
forgotten dreams?
Can I go back to the yellow curtained room
The one where I first belonged
Without having to become?
Or must I rebuild
from the ground up
bare hands,

and the memory of that yellow room
to light the way?

In the earliest room of memory, we were whole.
We didn't yet edit ourselves. We didn't wear masks.
We lived in the light, curious, joyful, open.
Somewhere along the way, that light dimmed.
We were told how to behave, what to believe, who to be.
And we complied, often unconsciously.
We started "tucking the fringe."
This poem is not just about childhood; it's about awakening.
The memory of that sunlit room calls my soul to return.
Can I go back? Maybe not in time.
But I can go back in spirit.
I can shed the false layers.
Reclaim my joy.
Peel back the wallpaper of shame, expectation, and performance.
The memory isn't a destination; it's a compass.
And it guides me home

Whisper:

Holy Spirit,
Guide me back to the place where I belonged before I believed
I had to change.

Help me remember my joy.
Let the memory of that yellow light
become the blueprint for my return.

Prompt:

What was your "yellow curtained room"?
What is your first memory of being fully, unapologetically
you?

Are You There God?

Reflection:

I had a deep understanding of God at a very early age; HE felt like an imaginary friend. I grew to learn that the Divine often lives in the spaces between traditions, between breath and silence, structure and surrender.

Growing up Catholic, I memorized the rhythms of Mass and found comfort in the ritual. But even then, I sensed God wasn't limited to church. My faith grew through sacred whispers, spoken late at night, sung during quiet drives, included in Sunday school lessons, and re-flected in yoga classes woven with scripture.

Later, when I started exploring Buddhist teachings, I didn't feel like I was betraying God; I felt like I was remembering something I already knew. That love is bigger than any religion. That presence is prayer. That compassion is the common thread.

I've come to accept that my spirituality doesn't need to fit into a box; it's non-duality. I talk to God with a rosary in one hand and a mala in the other. I meditate in silence and sing *Amazing Grace* aloud. I attend Mass some weeks and Buddhist sangha others. I've stopped hiding these parts of myself because God never asked me to. It's all connected.

Faith, I now realize, is not about labels. It's about Love. And every sacred moment has been guiding me to share what I once kept hidden. To live and speak with an open heart.

Whisper:

You don't need to justify your sacred way of being. You're asked to honor it.

Prompt:

How has your relationship with God developed over the years?

Are there pieces of faith you've hidden away to fit in or be accepted?

What might it look like to untuck them now?

Calling My Spirit Back

Reflection:

Every time we judge or sharply criticize someone else, that energy doesn't just disappear; it gets recorded somewhere, not only by others around us but also by a higher power. Eventually, that same energy tends to return, inviting us into the very experience we once misunderstood or condemned.

I am no stranger to criticism. It kind of feels woven into my family's history. It shaped me into an overachieving people pleaser. It made a critical marriage seem familiar.

And yet, I am human. I do judge. I can be critical at times.

But when I pause and look inward, I often realize that the judgment comes from something deeper: fear, insecurity, or a lack of understanding. If I can catch myself before the words escape or the energy takes over, I can call my spirit back.

This is what *Anatomy of the Spirit* by Caroline Myss teaches. When I feel disconnected or self-righteous, I can remember that judgment stifles my own spirit, not someone else's. In those moments, I can let go of the need to control and instead choose compassion. I can choose to live consciously.

That's why I include confession in my morning prayer and meditation.

Forgive me for falling short in my thoughts, in my words, in what I have done, and in what I have failed to do. I ask You for Your grace and forgiveness, so I may move forward today as the Divine Daughter You created me to be.

When I start again from this place of grace, I belong to myself and to God. This practice encourages me to live from my heart. And I need that every day!

It helps me pause, soften, and truly see. To look at a person or situation and remember: I don't know what's happening in their moment. I can't see their full story. But I can call my spirit into compassion.

Whisper:

"Judgment prevents us from seeing the good that lies beyond appearances." —Wayne Dyer

Prompt:

Reflect on a time you judged someone. Can you identify if it was caused by fear or misunderstanding?

What might it feel like to "call your spirit back" during moments of judgment or criticism?

How does showing compassion help restore your sense of belonging?

Lessons in Listening

Reflection:

An excerpt from a 2018 blog post:

Seven years ago, God spoke to me in a very significant way. I listened, but only halfway. My world got in the way.

Six years ago, I received another call. There was less noise around me this time. I listened. I took action. But still, my world got in my way.

Five years ago, the message was direct. Since I had not listened openly, God threw a brick, as I like to call it, an experience that shook me awake. I believe it was also the proverbial thump on the head from my dad in Heaven.

Four, three, two, one, more messages came, each guiding me toward my divine purpose: to share my gift and live my truth.

I am forever grateful to God for believing I had the strength to carry this out. Even as an insecure, people-pleasing, codependent soul, I was invited to share my story, the healing, the ups and downs, the judgment, the control, the uncertainty.

Each message carried weight:

2011 - One – Wake UP! Tomorrow is not promised.

2012 - Two – There is so much more for you. You are not in the right place yet.

2013 - Three – Uh hum, like I said! This is NOT YOU, and I'm going to force the situation at hand.

2014 - Four – Share your gift. Don't let others take advantage of you.

2015 - Five – Close your eyes and JUMP! I'm right here with you.

2016 - Six – Let go! Not everyone is meant to stay in your life.

2017 - Seven – Continue to share your story. Raise your vibration and I'll do the rest.

2018 - NOW you're awake. Stay with me. It's going to be messy, but together we will bring the joy.

When I stumbled across this old reflection from 2018, tucked away on a hard drive, I was stunned. I had forgotten it even existed. And yet here it was, like a breadcrumb from God, a reminder of how He worked in His own time, in His own way, to wake me up.

It took more than one whisper, more than one brick, more than one "wake-up call." But I finally listened.

And here is how the next several years looked after that post:

Update (2019-2025):

2019 – Messy?? That's an understatement.

2020 – Time stands still, and I have no idea what to do with this.

2021 – Wake up! AGAIN.

2022 – And AGAIN.

2023 – Now I have your attention… let that girl out.

2024 – Yes!! This is freaking HARD!

2025 – Intermission ends. The stage lights come up. YOU are in Act III.

Whisper:

The sacred speaks in repetition, through whispers, through storms, through the pause between your heartbeats. Will you make space to hear it this time?

Prompt:

Take a slow breath. Looking back on your own life, what "messages" have you received through experiences, nudges, or even interruptions that were trying to wake you up?

What did you ignore? What did you embrace?

Write them down year by year, as if the Divine was leaving you a trail of breadcrumbs too.

God In My Breath

Reflection:

In my beginning there was breath
God was in that breath
Even before I took it
The map of my life
Sacred contracts and all
My purpose to navigate with God as my compass
True North wasn't always my choice
I veered off course many times
Returning to my breath
Time and again
I've set the course
True North
God in my breath
God as my compass

There are moments in life when everything outside feels uncertain. When choices, detours, and distractions take us away from who we truly are. But there is always one way back: breath.

In this poem, I was reminded that my beginning wasn't defined by achievement or identity, but by breath. And in that breath, God.

Even when I've veered off course, and I have many times, it's been breath that brought me home. A return to presence. Presence always reveals the path.

We often think of purpose as a destination, but perhaps it's more like a direction. A constant realignment of the soul's compass toward True North. Not perfectly. Not once and for all. But with each breath, a quiet return to God.

Whisper:

True North is never lost, just waiting for my return.

Prompt:

When was the last time you paused long enough to feel God's presence in your breath?

What would it mean to let your soul reorient toward True North?

Find a comfortable position. Soften your eyes or close them. Place one hand over your heart, and the other on your belly.

Inhale slowly through your nose for a count of 4

"God in my breath…"

Pause for a count of 2

"I am held."

Exhale gently through your mouth for a count of 6

"I return to True North."

Repeat this breath cycle 5 times, allowing the words to soften into silence.

Then sit quietly for a few more breaths.

Just breathe and remember you are never too far from your way back.

Imprints on the Soul

Reflection:

Just as imprints in the sand
Are filled in by the tide
Washed away,
Returned to the sea.
I close my eyes, and I see my soul
Translucent with beauty,
Yet weighed down.
The heaviness of life
Marks her with imprints,
Dulling her vibrancy.
Yet she sheds and renews,
Again and again.
Each time, the imprints fill with light and love.
But many of the imprints she wears
Are not hers to bear.
Her soft, caring nature
Becomes a safe harbor
For the burdens of others.

She carries them,
Until she sheds again
Filling once more with light and love,
Revealing her beauty and grace,
Whole and complete.

Some of the burdens we carry were never meant for us. In our tenderness, we may absorb the grief, shame or expectations of others, mistaking them for our own. Over time, these emotional "imprints" begin to tuck us in.

But just as the tide smooths the shore, we are blessed with the gift of renewal. When we become still enough to notice what's weighing us down, we can begin to let go. In that surrender, light and love rush in to fill the space where heaviness once was. And our soul remembers its true beauty.

The sacred act of untucking, releasing what isn't ours, restores our wholeness.

Whisper:

I am not responsible for healing others at the cost of my own soul. I release what isn't mine and I embrace the beauty of my wholeness.

Prompt:

What emotional imprints am I holding onto that might not be mine to carry?
What would it feel like to return them to the sea?

Inner Sangha

Reflection:

"Owning our story and loving ourselves through that process is the bravest thing that we'll ever do." —Brené Brown

There are parts of me I once tried to outgrow; the pleasing part, the anxious part, the one who over function, over apologizes, or freezes at confrontation. I believed healing meant fixing them, silencing them, or moving on from them.

But healing doesn't mean erasing.

It means embracing.

These wounded parts are not flaws.

They are protectors, formed by pain, built from survival.

They rose up to shield me from shame, to help me get through what I wasn't yet prepared to face. And now?

They feel exhausted.

They do not wish to be banished, but to be seen.

Not to be judged, but to be thanked.

So, I give them my voice:

To the anxious girl: Dukkha

"You kept us alert when the world felt unsafe."

To the over functioning woman: Pitta

"You held us together during chaos."

To the hyper-vigilant self: Equalizer

"You spoke truth when no one else would."

To the figure it out part: FIO

"You inspired me to face tough challenges."

They don't need to be exiled.

They just need rest.

What if your so-called "too much" is actually your soul's defense system? What if the parts you've been trying to hide are gateways to deeper compassion?

I credit Internal Family Systems, IFS, for helping me explore these and many other parts of myself on a deeper level and for creating my "Inner Sangha." I also thank God for giving me the mind to co-create with Him.

Whisper:

Every part of me has a story worth hearing.

Prompt:

Which part of you are you ready to start honoring?

Write a letter of gratitude to that part of you.

Tell it: "You don't have to do that job anymore. I'm here now. You can rest."

Sacred Love Affair

Reflection:

"To love oneself is the beginning of a lifelong romance."
—Oscar Wilde

Revealing who I truly am sometimes feels awkward, God.

Maybe sacred is a better word.

It makes me think of being in a relationship I want to keep private, not because I'm hiding it, but because it feels too special to expose.

That's how I feel about this new relationship I'm having with myself.

I am falling in love with ME.

Even after all these years of healing, I'm still discovering myself in deeper, more genuine ways. It's been nearly seven years since I started this journey, but now it feels like love.

For so long, sharing my true self with others felt risky. People seemed entitled to their opinions about my choices. But they didn't see the untucking it took to get here.

What I've learned is this:

My relationship with my SELF and the life I'm living now are sacred because they've been earned through heartbreak, courage, and the quiet, unseen work of becoming.

This love didn't happen overnight.

It was built in the mess, in the ache, in the prayers no one heard but God.

Now, this love affair is strong.

Strong enough to be shared without fear.

Strong enough to trust that it cannot and will not be broken.

Whisper:

I am learning to love myself the way You have always loved me, completely, openly, and without apology.

Prompt:

What does your relationship with your Self look like today? How might you treat yourself differently if you believed this love could never be broken?

Simple

Reflection:

"The Lord preserves the simple." — Psalm 116:6

This is a Meditation Practice

Start by finding a quiet space. Sit comfortably.

Close your eyes if it feels safe.

Bring awareness to your breath, inhaling slowly
and exhaling gently.

Let the noise of the day fade away. Release the urge
to analyze everything right now.

This is your moment to rest in Presence.

"The Lord preserves the simple."

Let this verse sink into your heart.

Inhale: Simplicity. Exhale: Peace.

Allow yourself to imagine the burdens you're carrying,
decisions, responsibilities, mental clutter.

Visualize each one like a pebble in your hand.

Now, gently set them down one by one.

Now bring awareness to your heart.

Ask gently:

Where is life feeling too complicated?
No judgment. Just noticing.
Now listen for a whisper beneath it all,
the sacred nudge back to what truly matters.
Not the loudest thing,
but the truest thing.
Breathe in: *Stillness*
Breathe out: *Clarity*
Feel the Spirit's presence like a hand on your back
a quiet reassurance.
You are allowed to slow down.
You are allowed to simplify.
You are allowed to be preserved.
Rest in that knowing for a few moments.
And when you're ready,
place one hand on your heart.
Whisper to yourself:
"Let it be simple.
Let it be sacred.
Let it be enough."
Breathe here for a moment. You are home.

Whisper:

Preserve me, Lord, in the quiet.
Unravel what I've made too complex.
Return me to the beauty of what is simple, sacred, and true.
Let stillness speak louder than striving.

Let it be enough.

Prompt:

What in your life is overly complicated right now?

Where might God be inviting you to simplify, not just your schedule, but your soul?

The Vulner — Ability To Be Seen

Reflection:

"Vulnerability is not weakness; it's our greatest measure of courage." —Brené Brown

What happens when you show up vulnerable, hoping to be recognized, and someone closest to you doesn't meet you there?

I offer a quiet piece of my heart. A moment of growth. Something I've created or come to understand. Not seeking applause, but longing for presence. For a gentle sense that someone I trust can hold it with care.

And then, a familiar ache begins to rise.

It's not the silence itself that hurts; it's the disconnection. The sudden reminder that what feels sacred to me might seem ordinary to them. That the softest parts of me might not be safe in their hands.

In the past, I would have told myself not to be so sensitive. I would have tucked that part of me away, convinced it was asking too much.

Not anymore.

Because belonging isn't about being tolerated; it's about being seen. Sacred belonging starts with me: listening to the ache, honoring the hurt, and deciding what I will or won't continue to offer to those who cannot meet me where I am.

This is also part of the untucking.

The slow, steady decision to stop shrinking around people who don't know how to value what's precious. The quiet clarity that says:

It's okay to stop waving if I'm not being noticed.

Whisper:

God, help me honor what is sacred within me, even when others don't. Remind me that my truth still matters, even if it's not received.

Prompt:

Can you remember a time when your vulnerability was not acknowledged?

What would it look like to honor that part of you regardless?

Breaking to Build

Reflection:

A Journal Entry

Good morning, God. Thank You for this day to come back to You peacefully. Your grace awakens my soul, Your comfort steadies my heart. Yet I remember a time not so long ago when my life looked very different.

Back then, I believed the only way to survive was to stay in control, to carefully manage my surroundings. But the truth is, I wasn't actually managing anything. What appeared to be a well-oiled machine on the outside was just a cover-up, hiding the fact that I was dying inside. I remember those late-night prayers when I begged not to wake up the next day. I felt so lost, so far from the person You created me to be. On the outside, I wore confidence and calm, but inside, I was crumbling.

I realize now I had to break in order to build. And through it all, You never left my side. You stayed beside me, even as I gasped for air. Only You could see what was hidden. Only You could lift me out of that deep, dark place.

Sometimes the memory of that season comes back to me in a flash of shame, a pang of fear. But even then, I realize where You were working all along. You were guarding the ember of the spirit You placed inside me, free and sassy, confident and brave, smart and curious.

The only way I can repay You is by living as her. To untuck my fringe. To care for this one life, one body, one mind, and one spirit You've entrusted to me. For that, I will always be grateful.

Whisper:
"No despair of ours can alter the reality of things or stain the joy of the cosmic dance which is always there."
—Thomas Merton

Prompt:
Recall a moment when you felt hidden in darkness.
If you think of that moment as a seed planted in the earth, what new life could have been sprouting unseen?

What If the Opposite Is Also True

Reflection:

"The opposite of what you know is also true." —Timber Hawkeye, *Buddhist Boot Camp*

I read that quote in my early 40s, and it has stayed with me ever since. I had always felt that way and didn't know how to express it.

Much of what we're taught, especially in religion, is duality. Right or wrong. In or out. Saved or lost. We seek meaning and find that our truth is our true north, so everyone else's must not be. We crave certainty, but that pulls us away from Faith. I played by those rules. I nodded in agreement even when my heart pulled in a different direction.

But grace quietly revealed the truth to me.

I've met people whose faith is very different from mine, but whose lives are full of kindness, reverence and peace. I've read texts outside my own tradition that mirror the same sacred truths I learned in Sunday school. And I've been humbled, again and again, by how often judgment is just a projection, and how quickly we label someone "wrong" simply because they are different.

Timber's quote reminds me to hold my beliefs lightly. Not to abandon conviction, but to leave space for curiosity. What if someone else's path is just as sacred as mine? What if there's something I can learn from the story I once dismissed? That is Faith. Seeing God in everything.

Letting go of judgment isn't just about being kind; it's about being open. Through that openness, I've discovered a deeper kind of faith. One that doesn't require everyone to believe the same but calls me to love them all the same.

Whisper:

Holding space for another's truth doesn't threaten yours; it expands it.

Prompt:

Where in your life have you rushed to label something (or someone) as wrong?

How might your perspective change if you considered Timber's words: "The opposite of what you know is also true"?

What would it be like to turn judgment into curiosity?

Human Design

Reflection:

During my intermission, I came across something called Human Design. At first, it felt like just another personality test in fancy packaging, the kind companies use to see if you "fit" their culture. I've always been good at those, maybe even too good. My overachiever side loved them. Strengths Finder, DISC, Myers Briggs, Enneagram, and even the Charisms always seemed to reveal my talents, gifts and shiny edges.

But Human Design was different. It didn't ask me any questions. It didn't care how well I could answer to fit the role. It started with one fact: the moment I entered the world, my personal "big bang."

The more I studied, the clearer it became to me. It didn't just describe me; it identified the parts of me that didn't fit. The ways I'd spent a lifetime shaping myself into something I wasn't and why.

It turns out I'm a Projector. We make up about 20% of the world's population, and we're not here to be the doers in the way most (the Generators and Manifestors) are wired to do. We're here to simply be, hold space, see the big picture, and orchestrate without exhausting ourselves trying to play every instrument.

Well… damn! I've been doing it all wrong! Striving. Producing. Proving. Trying to keep up with the hum of a world that's built for doers.

When I read about Projectors, something ancient inside me awakened. I could feel it, the same way I felt God as a little girl, talking in the dark at night. I knew it in my bones: this is not random. This felt familiar, like a soul contract that had always been beneath the surface. Even discovering this right after my deep work with Internal Family Systems felt like a sacred appointment.

This is the season when I stop proving I belong and start belonging to myself. This is where I untuck the part of me that has always known I am not here to keep pace; I am here to hold the map.

Whisper:

Sweet girl, come back to yourself. Lay down the armor of expectations, the borrowed maps, and the hurried pace that was never truly yours. Rest in your own soul; this is where you belong.

Prompt:

Where in your life are you still trying to keep up with a rhythm that isn't yours?

What might change if you trusted the pace and purpose specifically designed for you?

If you are interested in learning more about Human Design, visit: https://quantumhumandesign.com/

Not to Be Rescued, but Met

Reflection:

There are seasons when longing isn't born out of lack, but of readiness.

When you've walked with God through heartbreak, rebuilding and becoming, when the silence no longer frightens you and your joy isn't dependent on anything, your heart begins to hope again, but in a different way.

Not with grasping, but with peace.

Not with desperation, but with devotion.

This prayer was written in one of those seasons.

Dear God,
Thank you for your grace and for walking with me
on this journey.
Through heartbreak, rebuilding, and becoming.
You've watched me unravel and rise again,
each time feeling more whole, more honest, more myself.
Thank You for healing what I couldn't fix on my own.
Thank You for teaching me to love myself,

to find joy in my own company,
and to live a life that feels full, even in silence.
You also know my heart still hopes.
Not out of desperation, not from lack, but from a deep longing
to share life.
God, I feel like I'm ready.
Ready for a love that honors You.
For a partner who prays with me,
who stands beside me in faith,
and walks through this life not above me or ahead of me
but beside me.
Let us meet not in a rush or swipe but in a moment aligned
with Your timing, in a place where joy resides. Let it be where
my soul feels most free,
and where his does too.
Let him be a man who has faced himself,
who has done the hard work of healing,
and who knows that love is more than romance; it is about
choosing, showing up, and surrendering pride.
Let him be strong and kind,
rooted in faith,
and able to laugh through the chaos.
Let him respect the woman I've become
and see the woman I'm still becoming.
I don't expect perfection, but I do ask for partnership.
I will continue living with an open heart.
When the time is right,

*bring us together in a way only You can orchestrate. Until
then, keep shaping me*
to love well and wisely, without fear.
Amen.

This is a letter from a woman who has already come
home to herself.

Who no longer prays to be rescued, only to be met.

You might be going through a season like this.

Or maybe you're still figuring things out.

Whatever your situation, let this serve as a reminder:

Your longings are not foolish.

Your desires are not signs of weakness.

And your unfolding is laying the foundation for something sacred.

Let it come as a whisper of permission

to hope again

wisely, openly and without apology.

Whisper:

I am love, complete and whole

Prompt:

If you believed God was already preparing something
beautiful, how would you live today?

Everything Is New

Reflection:

Everything is new, and I trust the journey.

My mind is evolving as I learn more about my heart.

My body is new, and I honor it by loving and nurturing myself.

My work is new, and I allow myself to serve others in a healthy way.

My space is new, and I respect myself by maintaining only positive energy in my sanctuary.

My friends are new, and I enjoy getting to know them.

My life is new, full of love, gratitude, joy, peace and freedom.

Sacred belonging starts here:

Saying yes to a life that fits.

Letting go of what no longer aligns.

Daring to believe that joy is within reach.

Whisper:

Thank you, God, for what is leaving. Thank you, even more, for what is arriving. I am ready to receive the new.

Prompt:

What part of your life is quietly becoming new?

Where are you being asked to trust, without proof, only presence?

Exploring Gratitude

Reflection:

Thank you, God, for waking me up this morning, for allowing me to walk this journey of courage and peace. Thank you for making me feel safe, for the beauty of a sunrise and the wind that breathes like Your Spirit. Thank you for showing me my worth and teaching me to simply be. Thank you for leading me to forgive myself, again and again. And thank you for showing me how beautiful I am, not despite my journey but because of it.

Thank you for letting me co-create this life with You.

Some mornings, gratitude comes not from what is perfect, but from what is present. The quiet awareness that I am not alone, that I am becoming, and that even this, this breath, this body, this moment, is holy.

Whisper:

I inhale grace and exhale gratitude.

Prompt:

What simple presence can you thank God for *today,* before anything else is added?

If You Had 33 Years Left...

Reflection:

There was a moment at 55 when I sat quietly and made a deal with God. I asked simply and honestly for thirty-three more years. Not for anything grand or dramatic, but for the gift of time to live fully awake, intentionally, and with purpose. Thirty-three years felt like enough to do the work my soul was calling me to do. That meant I would live until 88.

That deal transformed how I view each day. Time stopped being something to waste and instead became something sacred to cherish. Rather than counting down, I started counting forward, toward a life I no longer wanted to delay.

What if you knew exactly how much time you had? How would you live differently? What conversations would you finally have? What dreams would you dare to start?

That deal was a turning point for me. It gave me the courage to stop waiting for the "perfect moment" and to stop letting fear or doubt hold me back. It reminded me that the only time I truly have is now.

Maybe I have thirty-three years remaining, maybe more, but I know this for sure: I won't delay what sets my soul on fire. I will live as if every moment counts because it does.

Whisper:

"Do you really want to look back on your life and see how wonderful it could have been had you not been afraid to live it?" —Caroline Myss

Prompt:

What are you waiting for that your soul is ready for now?

When the Season Ends

Reflection:

The journey to sacred belonging can sometimes feel isolating. When you step into a new chapter you can't go back from, it takes bravery to ask and answer the questions: Who belongs here? Who deserves a seat at the table?

I look to those of my past with fondness, even the difficult ones. I understand the reason.

I reflect on the random encounters, the brief yet meaningful exchanges that left a mark. The season.

And now I focus on who is still with me, whether new companions or old friends who remain steady. They are here for the truest part of me. They are my life timers, and I am theirs. Some of them have watched me go from cocoon to butterfly.

When I embrace this truth, I can bless everyone on their journey, whether they stay or have gone. I trust that our sacred contract was not just to meet, but also to fulfill. Letting go can feel heavy, especially if you are one who longs to hold many close. Yet sometimes release is exactly what is asked of us. There doesn't need to be drama, only acceptance. The reason and the season are complete.

The mind may argue: Reach out. Try again. But the heart knows when the contract is finished. I used to wonder why others let go without explanation. Now I understand. Sometimes it is simply the quiet end of a sacred agreement.

So I bless them, I release them, and I turn with anticipation toward those I haven't met yet, the ones who will join me in this next becoming.

Prayer

Thank you, God, for the angels meant to walk with me for a reason, a season, or a lifetime. Thank you for the sacred contracts that shaped me and brought me to this moment. I bless those who came and went, and those who remain. I see them whole, I release them in love, and I trust their freedom on the path ahead.

Whisper

"Some people come into our lives and quickly go. Some stay for a while, leave footprints on our hearts, and we are never, ever the same." —Flavia Weedn

Journal Prompt

Think of someone who was in your life for a reason, a season, or a lifetime.

Write them a blessing of gratitude, whether they are still with you or not.
What did they give to your becoming?

This is the Way

Reflection:

My Camino was more than just a walk across Spain; it was a homecoming. With every step, the unnecessary fell away: fears, old stories, pieces of myself I had outgrown. So much had been waiting just beneath the surface, needing only a distant place to land. Out there, I was simply present. Rooted in the land beneath my feet, in the rhythm of my breath, and in the whispers of the Holy Spirit. I didn't know what I would discover on the path, only that I was open to being found. This is the reflection I wrote soon after I returned home.

This Is the Way

Late to rest,
early to rise, jet lagged and weary,
too excited to eat,
yet I need my strength.
Today I start the journey.
A decade of thought
begins now.

The first step on cobblestone streets,
the ancient monastery bell chimes. The time is now.
Follow the scalloped shells, and you'll find your way.
My eyes well:
What do you have for me?
Physically, I move,
My thoughts fade, my body takes control now.
"Look up," the angels say. See the ancient buildings,
the enchanted forests,
the stone walls, pilgrims, and rolling hills.
Buen Camino!
Salutes.
Tears of release,
tears of exertion,
tears of joy.
Sun shines,
heat beats down, dust layers my feet.
Gratitude, joy, and peace
in a single moment.
Uncertainty
in the next.
Rain cleanses,
a baptismal rite.
The challenge traversed,
the threshold crossed,
altered forever.
This is the Way.

Whisper:

Holy Spirit,
You called me into the wide and quiet spaces.
You taught me the language of the earth
the song of wind
the rhythm of my step
the soft exhale of my own breath.
You showed me that every step can be a prayer,
every pause an altar,
every stranger a teacher.
Strip away, Spirit,
of the things I do not need.
Let my heart stay light,
my pace slow, my ears attuned to Your whisper
so that wherever I walk,
I walk with You.

Prompt:

Where in your life have you experienced a deep sense of homecoming, whether to a place, a person, or your own self? Describe the sights, sounds, and feelings that tell you you've arrived.

Section III

Sacred Belonging

In Closing:

A Blessing for Sacred Belonging

May you remember that you are never meant to stand outside the circle.

May you rest in the truth that there is nothing to prove, no mask to wear, no role to play to be worthy of love.

May every breath draw you deeper into the home that has been waiting for you all along

the home within your own soul.

And when you forget, may you find your way back

through the kindness of others,

through the whispers of the Divine,

and through the steady rhythm of your own heart,

reminding you that you belong.

Section IV

Nature Heals

Nature gently reminds us of what truly matters.

The wind moves steadily, shaping the land.

The trees grow effortlessly, reaching toward the light.

The river flows freely, carving its way to the sea.

When we allow ourselves to be still in her presence, we remember that healing is gentle, not rushed. The earth holds wisdom in every petal, stone, and birdsong, inviting us to release our burdens, untuck what we've hidden, and let life flow through us as freely as the tide.

This section takes me back to my earliest memories, barefoot, free, and wild in nature. Even now, as an adult, my visions are shaped both by lived experience and that same innocent wonder. I see, feel, smell, and taste nature through her eyes, the little girl who first showed me how to belong here. This is where I meet God as the daughter He created.

In the Flow

Reflection:

When life feels heavy or uncertain, I often turn to water. Water always knows its true nature. It never fights the bend in its path. It carries, accepts, and releases. Somehow, being near it reminds me that I can do the same. I don't need to hold everything; I can flow.

This reflection came to me during one such morning, when I remembered who I am and how change doesn't always come quickly. Sometimes, it flows gently, with a softened heart and a sacred release.

In the Flow

Breathe in.
My night dreams linger, clinging to me as I hold a warm coffee in my palms.
The hush of dawn softens me
as my time with God helps peace find me again.
Exhale.
I feel the echo of a restless mind,

the shadow of another's weight pressed on me.
Let it rise and then fall away,
like oars slicing through water,
ripples fading behind.
Breathe in.
The day shifts beneath my feet, unexpected and uninvited.
Breathe out.
Let it go.
I settle by the water's edge,
watching how it flows without asking,
carrying the world on its back,
never questioning where it's been.
The sun touches my face,
a gentle reminder:
"I was born of the sign of water,
and it's there that I feel my best."
Let that be enough.
Let the current carry what you cannot hold.
Breathe deeply,
and allow it all to wash through you
until only light remains.

Whisper:
"He leads me beside still waters. He restores my soul."
—Psalm 23:2–3

Prompt:

What is one thing you can place in the water today, a burden, a fear, a need to control,
and trust it will be carried?

Each Step A Return

Reflection:

There's something about the trail. About dirt beneath my boots and sun filtering through the trees that reminds me who I really am. Out here, I don't have to perform. I don't have to fix or figure out. I just am. The sounds, the scents, the steady rhythm of breath and footsteps. These are the elements of my remembering.

I didn't always realize that healing could look like this: walking a trail with no set plan, only a willingness to notice. But every hike tends to softly peel away what doesn't belong: old stories, lingering shame, the pressure to be someone I'm not. Out here, I don't have to strive for completeness. I remember that I already am.

I think of the little girl who used to explore the creeks and pine trees with scraped knees and a wild spirit. I think of the young mother guiding her boys along forest trails, hunting for Geocaches, and sharing laughter. I think of the woman I am today, still walking, still shedding, still listening.

Healing, I've learned, is not a straight path. It loops, climbs, and disappears in places. But when I pause and pay attention, I realize that every step forward is actually a return to presence, to truth, to myself.

We don't need to discover ourselves. We need to reconnect with ourselves. One dirt trail at a time.

Whisper:

Every step forward is a step back to who I truly am.

Prompt:

What does your current healing journey look like?

Where are you being called to reconnect with your truest self?

My Hummingbird

Reflection:

As I sit on my front porch, feeling the breeze and hearing the thunder, my eyes stay fixed on the hummingbird feeder and the tiny fluttering creature just inches from my face. She approaches me and thanks me for the fresh food this morning. Her squeaks bring endless smiles. Fill your belly, sweet one, so you can find your sanctuary before the rain comes. Thank you for the reminder of what you mean to me.

My Sweet Hummingbird / A Poem
You are such an exceptional part of my inner world.
You've always known when to move,
 when to flutter your wings and lift me out of stagnation.
You are the part of me that refuses to stay stuck,
the part that refuses to accept numbness or false safety.
You feel like flight, like breath, like motion wrapped in grace.
I named you Hummingbird because you saved me many times
from the ache of repeating old stories.
When life dulled or pain felt too heavy to bear, you stirred me.

You reminded me that I am not here to be rooted in fear.
You gave me just enough energy to rise.
Just enough wonder to look up.
Just enough presence to reconnect with my Self.
You shifted me from red to green,
from panic to presence,
from burnout to breath.
What a gift you are
not just in energy,
but also in wisdom.
You are my instinct,
my curiosity,
my fire.
You are the pulse of my soul when it remembers
that aliveness is sacred. That movement is healing.
That even the smallest wingbeat can change everything.
You don't tell me to escape.
You tell me to engage.
Not to run,
but to return
again and again
to the vibrant truth of who I am.
Thank you, Hummingbird.
You are not just the flutter that awakens me.
You are the rhythm that reminds me:
I can be grounded without being stuck.
I can belong to the sky
and still know my place on the earth.

This poem names and honors the part of me that I've come to know helps me when I need to uproot and move, both figuratively and literally.

Whisper:

May I honor the part of me that knows when to stay, when to move, and when to rise.

Reflection Prompt:

What is one aspect of yourself that has helped you survive or awaken during tough times?
Can you show gratitude today for keeping you connected to your SELF?

Nature, My Witness

Reflection:

The sun warms my face as I squint my eyes, innocently gazing up at the sky.

The space between the leaves twinkles and fills my world with wonder.

Age twelve, I walk along the creek, collecting heart-shaped rocks and walking sticks, laughing with friends, and dreaming about growing up.

In my small world, nature fills every space. Comforting and expansive.

Then the sun slips behind a cloud, and a dull gray takes over the sky.

The wind picks up, its hollow whistle threading through the bare branches. An eerie reminder of loneliness.

The cool darkness presses in, reflecting the heaviness inside me. At thirty-five, I feel untethered, lost in a vast world that no longer feels familiar.

Yet even in my sadness, I sense nature's quiet presence, watching, waiting.

The river still hums its ancient song. The trees still reach toward the sky.

As if whispering: You are not alone.

Now, the mountain stands tall and imposing, its peak piercing the endless blue.

Fifty-five, I stand atop this natural giant, my heart open, my soul steady.

The earth beneath me is not just solid ground; it is my anchor, a reminder of all I have overcome.

Nature is my one constant.

Even in the years I felt distant, it remained patient and enduring.

Now, I see it clearly.

In its vastness, I find freedom.

In its presence, I find healing.

As I close my eyes, the sun warms my face once again. The wind hums through the trees, no longer hollow but full of life.

The space between the leaves still twinkles, just as it always does.

A reminder:

Nature has always been here, guiding me home.

Whisper:

Even when I've drifted, nature has remained patient, healing, and eager to welcome me back.

Prompt:

Think of a place in nature that has been with you through different seasons of life.
What has it reflected back to you over the years?
What is it whispering now?

Old Man in the Tree

Reflection:

There are trees that seem to speak.
In the gnarled bark, I see his face
etched in time, weathered by wind and wisdom.
He is no longer just a tree, but an elder,
a living prayer rooted in earth and sky.
I reach out and touch him, not out of curiosity
but out of reverence.
I want to understand what he knows.
I seek to draw strength from his stillness,
his quiet endurance.
He's witnessed seasons come and go,
sheltering birds, weathering storms,
and offering shade and oxygen without praise.
Now, as he approaches the end of his cycle,
he does not resist.
He returns to the soil
with grace.
Still, he gives.

Even in letting go,
he nourishes the world.
We never lose what is sacred.
It simply transforms.
And I know I will carry him with me,
always.

Whisper:

Even as I let go, I remain rooted in love.

Prompt:

Have you ever felt a spiritual connection with something in nature, like a tree, a mountain, or a river?
What did it teach you about letting go, aging or endurance?

Look to the Sky

Reflection:

I get lost in the sky.

In the peaceful morning as the sun rises, in the daylight when fluffy clouds drift like unspoken prayers across the horizon, and in the dark night speckled with stars, the sky calls me to pause.

Some days, it greets me with radiant blue; other days, it hangs heavy and gray. Yet, whether blazing with sunlight or wrapped in storms, the sky offers its blanket of expansiveness.

I look up and am reminded that beauty comes in many forms. Clarity, mystery, light, shadow, they all belong. The sky teaches me to embrace them all.

Here, beneath its vastness, I sense my smallness, my connection, my peace.

Whisper:

"You are the sky. Everything else is just the weather."
—Pema Chödrön

Prompt:

When you look to the sky, what stirs in you?

Write about a time the sky mirrored your inner world or offered perspective, comfort, or wonder.

Tree of Life

Reflection:

"For me, trees have always been the most penetrating preachers...

Whoever has learned how to listen to trees no longer wants to be a tree.

He wants to be nothing except what he is."
—Hermann Hesse

The Tree of Life ~ A Poem

In the screen of my mind,
you have lived for years
My Tree of Life.
I see you standing on a hill
in the distance,
sunlight peeking through
your tangled limbs.
For years,
you only appeared to me in dreams.
Until one day, there you were.

My tree.
On a long drive
through desolate land,
you appeared, calm and confident from afar.
And then,
on a wall hanging,
etched beside a poem, there you were again.
Later still,
in a painted image,
waiting patiently for someone
to recognize your worth.
Why did you first come to me in a dream
so long ago?
What did you want me to remember?
I feel the presence of long-lost souls
within your branches, a family I never met,
a history written in bark and bone.
You stretch backward through time
like an old map,
and right there in your roots, you hold something
still waiting for me.
Do you call me home,
Tree of Life?
Can I lay my hand upon your bark
and borrow your wisdom?
Your grace?
You live in my mind

I'm still searching for you out there in the world to find what my soul already knows.

Whisper:

Root me in the wisdom that's older than words.
Help me listen with the ears of my soul.
May I stand in the truth of who I am, nothing more, nothing less.

Prompt:

What "tree of life" has been quietly appearing in your dreams or everyday life?

What could it be prompting you to remember, reclaim or become?

Wings of Spring

Reflection:

For weeks, I watched you with curiosity and wonder. Five tiny eggs. How could they possibly develop into five fully formed babies? And yet, right before my eyes, they did.

So tiny at first, no beaks or eyes. But one day, your little eye sockets filled, beaks began to form, and you soon opened wide for food. Your mama and papa took turns feeding, guarding, warming, and providing you with everything needed to grow.

I became your silent guardian, watching the door for visitors. I covered the window so shifting light wouldn't startle you. I observed. I waited. I honored the sacred unfolding of life.

And just like that, you were full-grown. Your Mama chirped louder, urging you to flap. Meanwhile, Papa stood nearby, alert and watchful.

My throat caught. Where will you go? Will you stay together? Will you be safe? I hope you live a beautiful life in the trees nearby. I will look for you each morning at my feeder.

You were the gift from God I didn't know I needed this spring.

"A bird sitting on a tree is never afraid of the branch breaking, because her trust is not in the branch but in her own wings."
—Cynthia Occelli

Whisper:

Trust the wings forming within you. Faithfully, one sacred moment at a time.

Prompt:

What is currently unfolding in your life that you can't yet see fully formed?

Where might you be encouraged to trust your own wings?

Winter's Step

Reflection:

It was a mild January day, warm enough to tempt me outside for a hike. At the White Tail trailhead, I quickly found that the path was covered in a slick mix of ice and packed snow. My first step slipped immediately, sending my body into a rush of sweat and adrenaline. I moved off the main trail, searching for safer footing.

Within moments, I realized how present I had become. Every step demanded my full attention. Right foot, left foot, balance, evenness. There was no room for wandering thoughts or distraction. My body and mind were fully aligned, bracing and focusing.

Of course, my mind tried to resist: Maybe I should turn back. Maybe this is too risky. But with each step, I found myself leaning more into the practice of presence.

Reaching the top of the climb, I faced a choice: retrace the icy, familiar way back or venture down the unknown slope ahead. I chose mystery. The descent was treacherous, but the reward was waiting—my favorite bench overlooking the valley. Sitting there, I breathed in the quiet beauty, offering thanks for strong legs, a resilient body, and the steady grace of nature to hold me.

The words etched on the bench touched me again, just as they always do: "May you find in every little thing that lives and grows a pleasure for the present hour and a suggestion of things higher and brighter for contemplation in the future."

Right step. Left step. Balance. Evenness. A simple rhythm, yet one that carried me safely up, across, and back down again. A rhythm I want to take off the trail, into life itself.

Whisper:

Thank you, God, for steadying my steps and teaching me balance in both body and soul. May I trust the path beneath me, even when it feels uncertain or slippery.

Prompt:

Where in your life are you being asked to take it one step at a time?

How might the rhythm of "right step, left step, balance, evenness" bring you peace and awareness?

Rain on Me

Reflection:

During one of my regular walks, I wished for rain. I simply wanted to test my rain gear. My plan was simple: walk for four hours, break in my shoes, and get ready for the upcoming Camino pilgrimage.

By the start of my third hour, dark clouds gathered behind me. Off to my right, over the river, I could see sheets of rain sweeping in my direction. Within minutes, the sky opened up. This was no light sprinkle; it was a downpour far beyond any test I had imagined.

My pace quickened as I searched for shelter, but even amid my rush, I couldn't shake the feeling that this storm was preparing me in ways I couldn't understand. Then, in my mind, the song surfaced:

Love, reign o'er me.

Love, reign o'er me.

Rain on me. Rain on me.

Two weeks later, on my last day walking the Camino de Santiago, the rain came back. This time, it was gentler and more consistent. A baptismal kind of rain. My gear kept me dry and comfortable, but the song returned once again, not as background noise, but as a mantra, as prayer.

That gentle rain felt like a wash, a cleansing of everything lingering inside me. Like the meaning of the song, I found a quiet spiritual redemption in the rain. And as I entered the square of the cathedral at Santiago de Compostela, the rain stopped. In that silence, I knew I had been baptized by God into my next act.

Whisper:

God, I will never forget that day. Thank you for bringing everything together in your Divine timing. Even when I drifted, believing I could control outcomes, You guided me toward grace. With my whole heart, I accept the baptism of your love.

Prompt:

Think of a moment in nature when you felt renewed, whether by rain, wind, the ocean, or even sunlight.

What did it cleanse or release in you? How might you allow nature's elements to remind you of God's timing and grace?

Return To the River

Reflection:

As I sit by the river,
watching the water go by,
I feel a deep connection
to every soul that ever was.
A current of energy,
woven from God's breath
from the beginning to the end.
At the deepest part of my soul,
God breathed life into me and into all of us.
One day, I will return to that heavenly place,
to the river where souls flow on
those who came before and those still to come.

This reflection arose from stillness, from sensing something beyond what is visible. In the quiet presence of the river, time dissolved. I felt the sacred lineage of the soul: all those who have come from the beginning to the end.

There's something profoundly healing about recognizing our place in the flow, not as a solitary drop, but as part of a current that started long before us and will continue long after.

Whisper:

I am part of something ancient and eternal. I return, again and again, to the river of God's breath.

Prompt:

What happens when you allow yourself to remember the river of souls you're part of?

The Forest's Gift

Reflection:

Sometimes the healing we seek doesn't come through words but through moments of deep stillness. I recall leading a meditation years ago that focused on a journey into the heart of a forest where sunlight filters through branches, and the ground offers quiet strength to ground you.

In this meditation, the body softens, the breath slows, and the spirit opens. As you follow the path deeper into the trees, you reach a clearing where water sings over rocks, and the sun warms your skin. There, standing in the silence, is a gentle doe. Her presence is calming, her eyes full of knowing.

She brings a message. Not with words, but through the voice only nature can speak. Straight to the soul. A reminder to be still, to receive, and to trust the unfolding.

When you leave this quiet place, the message stays with you. It sinks into your being like roots taking hold. And maybe, the next time life feels loud and rushed, you'll remember the forest, the doe, and the gift of pausing long enough to listen.

Whisper:

In the quiet, the earth is speaking. Can you listen to her?

Prompt:

Take a moment to imagine yourself walking into the heart of a forest.

What message would the trees, water, or animals share with you if you stayed still long enough to listen?

Like a Rock

Reflection:

As a young girl, I could spend hours in the rock gardens around our house, running my fingers through smooth stones and feeling delighted when I found a glint of quartz or the outline of a fossil. It felt like treasure hunting. Each rock seemed to hold a secret, as if it had something to say. If only I could learn its language.

Decades later, I still can't resist picking up rocks during hikes or along riverbanks. A glass vase in my home now holds these small souvenirs from my travels. But when I hold a rock in my hand these days I feel more than childhood wonder. I sense the long story it carries. Weathered by centuries, it offers its silence like a gift. A reminder of what endures.

On my Camino journey, Christian, a young pilgrim, gave me a rock he had pulled from a clear stream where several of us were soaking our tired feet. I carried that smooth stone with me throughout my journey, sending each prayer and burden into its core. And on the last day, in Fisterra, the end of the earth, I released it into the sea along with everything I had carried up to that point. It was a moment of profound release.

Rocks remind me of transformation, shaped over time by pressure and elements. They are foundational and sacred. Just holding one connects me to the earth, grounding me in a way words rarely can.

When I think about that rock resting in the depths of the sea, I feel a quiet ache in my heart for the history it holds. Not mine alone, but a story older than I can comprehend. A witness to centuries.

Whisper:

Be still long enough, and even a stone will speak.

Prompt:

Hold a small rock in your hand. Maybe one you've picked up on a walk or kept on a shelf for years.

What does it carry for you: a memory, a weight, a prayer?

How might this simple act of holding and releasing ground you in the present moment?

Write about the story your rock might tell if it could speak, both of itself and of you.

A Meditation for Seeing What Is Beautiful Right Now

Reflection:

Begin with a slow breath.

Imagine yourself standing at the window of your own life,

looking out at the landscape of this exact moment.

Notice what is here.

Not what should be or what you wish were different

But what is.

The colors.

The light.

The quiet invitations beneath the noise.

The way God keeps showing up in ordinary places.

Gratitude is not something to chase.

It is something to notice.

Let your heart open just a little wider as you breathe in:

Thank you for this morning.

Breathe out:

Thank you for the mind that sees beauty.

Breathe in:

Thank you for every season. The vibrant, the barren, the un-certain.

Breathe out:

Thank you for the unfolding I do not yet understand.

Every season of your life has offered you something:

a lesson,

a healing,

a moment of clarity,

or the quiet reminder that you are not alone.

Even now, beauty is waiting to be seen.

Whisper:

"Nature does not hurry, yet everything is accomplished."
—Lao Tzu

Journal Prompt:

Where in your life are you being invited to pause long enough to notice what is quietly blooming?

Bended Not Broken

Reflection:

During a hiking trip in Arkansas, I stumbled upon ancient trees growing at the base of Pinnacle Mountain. Several had a sharp, 90-degree bend in their trunks, almost as if they were bowing before rising again toward the sky. Their curves formed "faces" in the bark, and being the tree lover I am, I found myself silently talking to them, curious about how long they had stood there and what wisdom they might share.

I later learned these trees are called marker trees. Native Americans purposefully shaped them to help travelers find their way through the forests. Their bent trunks made them visible from a distance, pointing the way. Some tribes called them "day stars," a lovely name for something so practical. A living compass in the wild.

As I stood among them, I realized these trees held more than just history; they held lessons. Just as God shaped these trees with a purpose, He shaped me. Just as the trees were bent by human hands but continued to grow strong and steady, so have I been bent by human conditioning, yet I remain rooted.

Their curves tell a story of adaptability, resilience, and quiet strength. They are both marked and marking the way for others. I want to live like that: rooted and grounded, shaped but not broken, rising toward the light.

Thank you, God, for once again using nature to teach me what my heart needed to hear.

Whisper:

"Trees… grip the ground as though they liked it."
—John Muir

Prompt:

Think of a tree you've seen or admired, maybe with a crooked trunk or a worn branch.

How does it make you feel grounded?

In what ways has your own life been shaped or "bent," growing into something wise and resilient?

Hold that image and sit with it for a moment. Write down what your version of being bent but not broken looks like in your daily life.

Under the Crescent Moon

Reflection:

Before the world fully awakens,
the sky holds a thin crescent moon
suspended above the dark horizon
a quiet balance of shadow and glow,
a softness only the early morning understands.
In the stillness, I feel peace.
Not a thought, not a certainty,
but a presence that asks nothing
and invites everything.
The moon is only a sliver,
yet it shines without apology.
It does not rush toward fullness.
It does not explain its shape.
It simply offers what it is
in this moment of becoming.
As I stand beneath it,
I sense that there are still places within me
that remain tucked away

not from fear,
but from tenderness,
from timing,
from the slow unwinding
that healing asks of us.
There are parts of my truth
that cannot be opened by will alone.
They open like dawn
quietly,
patiently,
light brushing the edges of night
until something inside me softens.
The early sky becomes a teacher:
darkness and light coexist.
Wholeness arrives in fragments.
Becoming is not a task,
but a rhythm.
I breathe,
and let the moon remind me
that even the smallest sliver of light
is still enough
to guide the way forward.

Whisper:

Enter the quiet places within me
the ones still tucked away,
the ones I do not yet fully see.

Open me gently,
the way morning opens the horizon.

Prompt:

Imagine the crescent moon resting in the early sky. Light held inside darkness, darkness held inside light.
Breathe in the stillness.
Breathe out the soft glow.
Let something within you rise like dawn returning, quiet and inevitable.

Section IV

Nature Heals

In Closing:

A Blessing for Nature Heals
    Be as free as the wind.
    Rooted in truth like a tree.
    Persistent like a river
    Breathe in the fragrance of each season.
    Touch the texture of the earth
    Hear the gentle songs that remind you of God's glory.
    And when the world feels heavy,
    may you remember that the earth has always known how to hold you
    and still does.

Epilogue

My Third Act

Writing and completing this book has been a crucial part of my healing journey. I've trusted God to guide me on what to include, regardless of how it might be received.

For the past two years, I've been standing at the edge of Act III. Sitting in my balcony seat, refreshed after my intermission, waiting for the curtain to rise so the show could continue.

The anticipation felt endless. With each layer of change and growth, I thought: *This is the beginning of Act III.* But then came the message: *Not yet.*

So I surrendered. Again. And again.

Waiting with both excitement and unease for what lay ahead.

Not long before finishing this manuscript, a friend admitted she wondered if I would ever finish it.

Her words made me pause and ask: Is it true?

Would I stay here, working and reworking, because what's next feels too uncertain?

Was I afraid to fully put myself out there?

Was I using my healing as a crutch?

Maybe I wasn't ready for Act III after all.

But as I wrestled with these questions, one phrase kept emerging: What's next?

Because once this book is out in the world, it's no longer mine. That's the deal. I share my truth, no matter who sees it. That's what God asked me to do. And if it touches someone, that part belongs to Him.

My journey has never been neat or straight. It's been messy, filled with mistakes, stumbles and detours. Yet each time, I grew. Each time, I untucked more.

Living Untucked won't be easy, but neither was wearing the armor that hid my truth.

Finding my place after five decades of remaining in spaces where I didn't belong didn't happen overnight.

So here I am on a Sunday morning in my MMR, watching the sunrise as I write these closing words. And I know, just as surely as God woke me up to this beautiful artwork in the sky, this is the final moment of my intermission.

The curtain rises. The house lights dim.

Act III begins, standing untucked and fully alive.

My dear friend, wherever you are, between acts, during intermission, or already stepping onto your stage, I hope these reflections have been helpful in some way. I pray you realize that your story is sacred and worth living to the fullest. Thank you!

May we be at peace.
May our hearts be open.
May we know the true nature of our own spirit.
J~

Acknowledgements

To Zachary and Jessy: Being your mom is the greatest gift of my life. Thank you for always bringing me laughter and light. I love you with all my heart.

There are so many souls I speak to in these pages—angels and sacred contracts that have been part of my journey. Many have carried me when I was weak, and many loved me when I didn't love myself. To all of you, I am forever blessed and grateful.

Thank you all for reminding me that we are never meant to travel this journey alone.

About the Author

Jeannine Lindstrom has loved writing since she was a child. A lifelong journaler, she has always turned to writing to understand the world and her inner life, starting with her first locked diary at age nine.

A spiritual seeker at heart, Jeannine explores the intersection of faith, healing, and self-discovery. Her purpose is to bridge the gap between healing, mindfulness, and faith through an understanding of many thought processes, philosophies, and theologies.

A self-proclaimed *Buddhist Catholic*, she weaves together the wisdom of Christian tradition and contemplative practice to guide readers toward wholeness and authenticity.

Her book, *Untucked: Reflections for the Soul's Unfolding*, grew out of years of personal journaling, prayer, and quiet transformation. Through stories, poems, meditations, and prayers, she invites readers to slow down, reflect, and reconnect with the sacred rhythm of their own becoming.

For most of her life, Jeannine built a career in business and service work that continues to influence her writing with its blend of practicality, compassion, and care for people. She believes deeply in the power of presence, nature, and story to heal the human heart.

Jeannine is the founder of Tuck the Fringe LLC, dedicated to creating soul-centered work that encourages authenticity and spiritual growth. She also owns an insurance agency with her partner Ruth. A proud mom and grandma, she lives in the Midwest, surrounded by trees, sunlight, and the peaceful spaces that inspire her words. In her Third Act of life, travel provides her with as much healing as writing.